Council Tax Handboc

GW00786646

1st edition 1993–94

Martin Ward

CPAG Ltd
1–5 Bath Street London EC1V 9PY

Published by CPAG Ltd
1–5 Bath Street, London EC1V 9PY

© CPAG Ltd 1993

A CIP record for this book is available from the British Library

ISBN 0–946744–53–X

Production by David Williams Associates, Cambridge
Cover and design by Devious Designs, 0742 755634
Typeset by Bookman, Slough
Printed by Longdunn Press, Bristol

Contents

Acknowledgements

Special thanks go to Jim Read who has made a significant contribution to the handbook. I would also like to acknowledge the helpful comments of Lynda Bransbury, and Jim Gray of Drumchapel Law and Money Advice Centre, Glasgow. Additional thanks go to Peter Ridpath, David Williams, Derek Derbyshire, Alison Austin and John Halder who helped with this production.

Martin Ward
Information and Training Services
September 1993

How to help make the next edition better

Comments about errors or suggestions for points you would like to see in future editions of the *Council Tax Handbook* are welcomed. These should be sent to:

Martin Ward
Information and Training Services
P.O. Box 2244
London NW10 5DW

or to:

Council Tax Handbook
c/o CPAG Ltd
1–5 Bath Street
London EC1V 9PY

CHAPTER ONE

Overview

This chapter:

- introduces the council tax in England, Wales and Scotland and the council water charge in Scotland;
- identifies the appropriate administrative authorities;
- summarises the main features of the tax; *and*
- identifies the relevant legal and other sources.

From 1 April 1993 the council tax replaces the community charge ('poll tax') as the way in which local people in England, Wales and Scotland make contributions towards the cost of local authority services. Additionally in Scotland the council water charge replaces the community water charge as the means of payment for a public supply of water to a dwelling. This handbook details the council tax as it operates throughout Great Britain and the council water charge scheme as it operates in Scotland. It should be of value to administrators, advisers and taxpayers.

There are numerous differences in the detail of the schemes that operate in the different countries. In some chapters these are indicated as they arise, in others there are separate sections on the different arrangements. Domestic rates are still payable in Northern Ireland. This handbook, therefore, does not apply to Northern Ireland.

Administration

In England and Wales, the district councils, metropolitan districts and London boroughs, the Common Council of the City of London and the Council of the Isles of Scilly are responsible for setting the council tax, as well as billing and collection in their area. They are known as 'billing authorities'.[1]

In Scotland, the islands, regional and district councils all set an appropriate council tax. The billing and collection of the tax, however, is carried out by 'levying authorities'. The levying authorities are the islands and the regional councils.[2] Levying authorities are also responsible for collecting the council water charge where water is not supplied wholly by meter or the water authority is not under an obligation to provide it free of charge. There is no English or Welsh equivalent to the Scottish water charge. All rules applying to the council tax in Scotland also apply to the council water charge with the exception that the council water charge is not taken into account in the calculation of transitional reduction; and is not an eligible cost for council tax benefit purposes.

Arrangements may be made between a regional council and a district council, Scottish Homes or a new town development corporation for the latter bodies to carry out aspects of council tax administration including the administration of council tax benefit.[3]

In this handbook the term 'authority' is used to refer to both billing and levying authorities.

Chapter summary

The following paragraphs provide a structured overview of the scheme and the related chapter in the handbook which describes each aspect of the scheme in greater detail.

Dwellings (Chapter 2)

The council tax is a tax on domestic property known as 'dwellings'. Not all properties in a billing or levying authority's area count as dwellings. A property that is not a dwelling is usually subject to non-domestic rates. In England and Wales it is the valuation officer at the local valuation office of the Inland Revenue, and in Scotland the local assessor appointed by the regional or islands council, who decides whether or not a property is a dwelling. An appeal may be made against the decision that a property is, or is not, a dwelling.

Valuation (Chapter 3)

The government has attempted to relate the amount people have to pay in council tax to their ability to pay by relating it, in the first instance, to the assumed value of their dwellings. Dwellings are allocated to one of the eight valuation bands by the local valuation office or local assessor. Information about the dwelling and its valuation band appears on valuation lists maintained by the listing officer at the local valuation office and local assessor. The public have the right to inspect and obtain copies of the valuation list.

Proposals may be made for a change in, and appeals can be made against, a dwelling's valuation band.

The amount of tax (Chapter 4)

The amount of council tax payable varies between, and in certain instances, within authorities. Prior to the start of each financial year (April–March) each authority must set an amount of council tax that enables it to meet its budgeted expenditure and the budgeted expenditure of certain related bodies. For example in England and Wales the county council raises money via the district council's council tax while in Scotland the regional council also collects the district council's council tax. In certain instances the amount of money that may be raised through the tax may be restricted by central government.

The council tax payable on each dwelling in the authority depends, in the first instance, upon which valuation band it has been allocated to. Different valuation bands apply in England, Wales and Scotland. These reflect the different range of property prices in the three countries. There are a number of ways in which the council tax payable on a particular property may be reduced and these are examined in the next chapters.

Exempt dwellings (Chapter 5)

Certain categories of dwelling are on the valuation list but exempt from the tax. The exemption may be either indefinite or for a fixed period. No council tax is payable while the dwelling is exempt. An appeal may be made against the authority's refusal to grant an exemption.

Liability (Chapter 6)

The council tax is usually payable by someone aged 18 or over who is solely or mainly resident in the dwelling. Where there is more than one such person the liable person is the one with the greatest legal interest in the dwelling. Normally it is the owner, or the tenant, who must pay the council tax. However in particular circumstances a non-resident owner may be liable instead of a resident.

Where the liable person is married, or has an unmarried partner of the opposite sex, the partner is normally jointly liable for the council tax even if he or she has no legal interest in the dwelling. Also where two or more people, other than partners, have the same legal interest in the dwelling they may all be jointly liable for the council tax. Special rules apply where a liable person or partner is severely mentally impaired.

The authority has the right to obtain information from a variety of sources to identify liable individuals. An appeal may be made against the authority's decision regarding liability.

Disability reductions (Chapter 7)

The council tax payable on a dwelling may be reduced where the dwelling has certain features which meet the particular needs of someone who is substantially and permanently disabled. Annual applications must be made for these reductions. An appeal may be made where the authority refuses to award a disability reduction.

Discounts (Chapter 8)

In the first instance the council tax bill is based on the assumption that there are two or more residents aged 18 or over in the dwelling. Where there are more than two the bill does not increase but the bill may be reduced by:

- 50 per cent where the dwelling is no one's sole or main residence; *or*
- 25 per cent where it is only one person's sole or main residence.

Welsh authorities, however, have the discretion to only give a 25 per cent or zero discount on second homes. In deciding how many people are solely or mainly resident in the dwelling certain categories of people are disregarded. The authority must consider whether a discount applies in any particular case. Appeals may be made against the authority's decision not to apply a discount.

Transitional reduction (Chapter 9)

Transitional reduction schemes in England and Scotland help certain people who face significant increases in their bill as a result of the change from community charge to the council tax. There is no transitional reduction scheme in Wales. Appeals may be made against the amount of transitional reduction granted or an authority's refusal to grant such a reduction. These appeals should be made to the authority's benefit review board.

Council tax benefit (Chapter 10)

Additional assistance is available to meet the council tax in the form of council tax benefit (CTB).

CTB is one benefit but it takes two forms:

- main CTB; *and*
- alternative maximum CTB – more commonly referred to as second adult rebate.

Main CTB may be awarded in addition to the other forms of assistance already identified. If the claimant, together with any partner of the opposite sex, has capital of more than £16,000 that counts for benefit purposes he or she is excluded from assistance. The benefit calculation is based upon the claimant's council tax liability less any award of a disability reduction, discount or transitional reduction. It is also based on the claimant's (and any family's) assumed needs and resources. Main CTB provides up to 100 per cent help with the council tax where the liable person is on income support or a low income. The amount is reduced, however, if:

- the claimant is jointly liable for the council tax with someone other than a partner of the opposite sex;
- a non-dependant, such as an adult son or daughter, lives with the claimant; *or*
- the claimant's (and any partner's) income is above income support levels.

Second adult rebate is based on the income of certain other adults who live with the claimant but not the claimant's partner or someone who is jointly liable for the council tax. Claimants with any amount of capital or income may be entitled to second adult rebate. In certain instances rebates of up to 25 per cent of the claimant's council tax are available.

Applications must be made and periodically renewed for CTB. An application for CTB is also an application for second adult rebate. If the claimant is entitled to both main CTB and second adult rebate the authority should award whichever is the greater. Appeals may be made to the authority's benefit review board about both the amount of any CTB that has been awarded and the authority's refusal to award CTB.

Bills and payments (Chapter 11)

The council tax is not payable until a demand notice (bill) has been issued. Liability for the council tax arises on a daily basis throughout the year but bills are raised on the assumption that the circumstances they are based on will remain the same throughout the year. Where this is not the case they may be adjusted and in certain circumstances the taxpayer has the right to receive a refund of any overpayment.

People have a right to pay their council tax in instalments. This will usually be ten each year, but where liability to pay commences part way through the year the number of instalments is reduced. Authorities may also offer council tenants up to 52 instalments so that they are able to pay their council tax with their rental payments. Authorities also have the power to enter into special payment arrangements with individual taxpayers and to offer discounts for lump-sum payments and the adoption of non-cash payment methods.

Enforcement (Chapter 12)

The authority may use a variety of measures to ensure that a liable person pays the tax and any related costs and penalties. These methods range from the issuing of reminders to the taking of legal action. Such legal action enables the authority to:

- make deductions from the debtor's earnings;
- seize and sell the debtor's goods; *and*
- request the local social security office to make deductions from the debtor's income support.

In addition English and Welsh billing authorities, but not Scottish levying authorities, may apply to the magistrates' court for a warrant committing the debtor to prison. In all these circumstances the debtor has certain duties but also certain rights.

Appeals (Chapter 13)

Many decisions to do with the council tax have appeal rights attached to them. These may be categorised as appeals on matters to do with:

- valuation;
- liability;
- completion notices; *and*
- penalties.

Appeals on matters to do with property valuation should go first to the listing officer or the local assessor. Where the proposed change is not agreed to the case should automatically go forward to a valuation tribunal in England and Wales or a valuation appeal committee in Scotland.

Appeals on matters to do with liability, including the amount of tax payable on the dwelling, should first be addressed to the authority. This includes matters such as whether or not the aggrieved person is in fact liable to pay the tax or whether or not a disability reduction or discount should be awarded. If the authority fails to respond within two months, or the aggrieved person is still dissatisfied, a further appeal may be made to a valuation tribunal in England and Wales and via the levying authority to a valuation appeal committee in Scotland.

In England and Wales the authority, and in Scotland the assessor, may issue a completion notice that states the date on which a newly erected or structurally altered property is considered to be a dwelling. In England and Wales an appeal against the completion date must normally be made direct to the valuation tribunal within four weeks of the notice being sent. In Scotland an appeal to the valuation appeal committee must be made via the local assessor within 21 days from receipt of the completion notice.

There are various circumstances in which people may have to pay a penalty if they fail to provide information. Appeals against the imposition of penalties may be made directly to the valuation tribunal in England and Wales or via the authority to a valuation appeal committee in Scotland.

Legal background and references

The legal framework for the council tax is contained within the Local Government Finance Act 1992. The Act includes sections and Schedules that apply throughout England and Wales, and Scotland, as well as sections and Schedules that apply exclusively to one or other of the two jurisdictions.

The Act also enables the appropriate Secretary of State to formulate delegated legislation – statutory instruments – which contain and amend the details of the schemes. Different sets of statutory instruments apply to England and Wales and to Scotland. Additionally certain statutory instruments only apply to England or Wales.

Relevant case law is also identified in the appropriate paragraphs of the handbook.

Future changes

This handbook is up to date as the law stood on 1 July 1993. Changes will no doubt be made to the council tax and will be reflected in future editions of the handbook.

DoE Practice Notes

In addition to the legislation the Department of the Environment, the

Welsh Office and the local authority associations have together
produced a series of Practice Notes. These are listed in Appendix 3.
They advise on interpretation of the legislation, on administrative
arrangements and highlight a number of good practice points. There
is no Scottish equivalent. While the legislation is binding upon
authorities the Practice Notes do not have the force of law and are
not something that authorities have to have regard to. Particularly
useful comments from the Practice Notes are identified in this
handbook.

Notes in the handbook

References to the law are given in notes to each chapter at the end of
the handbook. The notes usually contain references to English and
Welsh law – denoted by the letters EW – followed by reference to the
equivalent Scottish provision – denoted by the letter S. The following
abbreviations are used in the notes:

- Act means the Local Government Finance Act 1992;
- 's', 'ss' and 'Sch' refer to the appropriate section, sections of, and
  Schedule to, the Act. For example EW Act s 11(1) refers to
  subsection 1 of section 11 in the Local Government Finance Act
  1992. The section applies to England and Wales only.
- EW A&E means the Council Tax (Administration and Enforce-
  ment) Regulations 1992, SI 1992 No. 613 which applies to
  England and Wales. This is followed by a reference to a 'Reg' or
  'Sch' number which identifies the specific Regulation or Schedule in
  the statutory instrument. For example EW A&E Reg 43(1)–(4)
  refers to paragraphs (1) to (4) of Regulation 43.
- S A&E means the Council Tax (Administration and Enforcement)
  Regulations 1992, SI 1992 No. 1332 (S 129) which applies to
  Scotland. Again this is followed by reference to a 'Reg' or 'Sch'
  number which identifies a specific Regulation or Schedule in the
  statutory instrument. For example S A&E Reg 9(1)–(4) refers to
  paragraphs (1) to (4) of Regulation 9.
- SI followed by a year and a number refers to the specific statutory
  instruments listed in Appendices 1 and 2. For example S SI 1992
  No. 1329 (S 126) refers to the Council Tax (Valuation of
  Dwellings)(Scotland) Regulations 1992.

References to chapters and pages in the main text of the handbook
are to other chapters and pages where a term or concept is defined or
discussed further. References to Practice Notes followed by a number
and a paragraph or page number are references to the Council Tax
Practice Notes mentioned above.

Legal and other references

Appendix 1 lists all the legislation currently available for England and Wales. Appendix 2 lists all the legislation currently available for Scotland. Appendix 3 lists all the English and Welsh Council Tax Practice Notes. No equivalent Practice Notes exist for Scotland.

CHAPTER TWO

Dwellings

This chapter explains:

- on which dwellings the tax must be paid;
- what counts as a dwelling in England and Wales;
- when one property can count as more than one dwelling or a multiple property only makes up one dwelling;
- what counts as a dwelling in Scotland;
- when a new or altered building becomes a dwelling; *and*
- how an appeal may be made against the valuation officer's or assessor's decision about a property.

Council tax is payable in respect of all dwellings which are not exempt (Chapter 5). Properties on which the tax must be paid are referred to as 'chargeable dwellings'.[1] For the purpose of determining for any day whether any property is a chargeable dwelling the state of affairs at the end of the day is assumed to have existed throughout that day.[2] Whether or not a property is a dwelling is one of the grounds for making a proposal for the alteration of the valuation list (Chapter 3) and could then be the subject of an appeal (Chapter 13).

What counts as a dwelling in England and Wales?

In England and Wales a dwelling is any property which:

- would have been a hereditament (ie a unit of accommodation) for the purposes of the General Rate Act 1967; *and*
- is not shown or required to be shown in a local or a central non-domestic rating list; *and*
- is not exempt from local non-domestic rating; *or*
- is a composite hereditament.[3]

Houses, flats, bungalows, cottages and maisonettes all normally count as dwellings. Caravans and houseboats may also count as dwellings. The council tax is charged on the pitch occupied by a caravan, or a mooring occupied by a boat. For council tax purposes a 'caravan' is anything that meets the definition contained within Part I of the Caravan Sites and Control of Development Act 1960. Holiday caravans and other caravans used for non-domestic purposes are subject to non-domestic rates.

Properties exempt from non-domestic rating

The properties that are exempt from local non-domestic rating are:

- agricultural buildings and land;
- buildings and land used solely for, or in connection with, fish farming;
- places of religious worship;
- lighthouses and certain other property of Trinity House;
- sewers;
- property of drainage authorities;
- certain property used by the disabled;
- air raid protection works;
- swing moorings; *and*
- property in enterprise zones.

Composite hereditament

A property is a composite hereditament if only part of it is used wholly for the purpose of living accommodation. For example some rooms in a property may be used only for business purposes while others only for domestic. Council tax is payable on the domestic portion and non-domestic rates are payable on the business portion. The false determination that a property is a composite hereditament gives grounds for appeal as does an incorrect determination as to the appropriate proportions of a property that are used for domestic and non-domestic purposes.

Properties that are not dwellings

In addition to non-domestic properties and the non-domestic proportion of a composite hereditament, none of the following count as a dwelling unless it forms part of a larger property which is itself a dwelling:

- a yard, garden, outhouse or other land or buildings belonging to or enjoyed with property used wholly for the purposes of living accommodation; *or*
- a private garage which either has a floor area of not more than 25 square metres or is used wholly or mainly for the accommodation of a private motor vehicle; *or*

- private storage premises used wholly or mainly for the storage of articles of domestic use.

Exclusion of Crown exemptions

Normally where the owner of a dwelling is the Crown it would not be liable to pay the council tax. The rules as to Crown exemption do not, however, prevent a dwelling provided and maintained by certain authorities for purposes connected with the administration of justice, police purposes or other Crown purposes from being a chargeable dwelling.[4] The authorities in question are:

- a billing authority other than the Council of the Isles of Scilly;
- a county council;
- a metropolitan county police authority;
- the Northumbria Police Authority;
- the Receiver for the Metropolitan Police District; *and*
- a combined police authority.

Dwellings situated in two or more authorities or different parts of the same authority

The location of a dwelling is a major determining factor in how much council tax is payable. Different authorities have different levels of council tax for dwellings in the same valuation band (Chapter 4). Additionally, where there are parish or community councils, different parts of the same authority may have different levels of council tax for dwellings in the same valuation band. Clearly in certain circumstances it will be advantageous for the liable person to assert that the dwelling is in one authority, or part of an authority, rather than another.

Where a dwelling falls within the area of two or more authorities, or two or more parts of an authority's area, it should be treated as situated in the area in which the greater or greatest part of the dwelling is located.[5] Where a dwelling is part of a single property which falls within two or more authorities, or two or more parts of an authority's area, it should be treated as located in the area in which the greater or greatest part of the property is located.[6]

When can one property consist of more than one dwelling?

Where a single property contains more than one part which has been constructed or adapted for use as separate living accommodation each unit of accommodation should be treated as a separate dwelling.[7] An interested person may make a proposal to the listing officer not to show his or her home as a separate unit of accommodation on the valuation list. The process of making a proposal is described in Chapter 3.

When does a multiple property constitute one dwelling?

The listing officer has the discretion to treat what would otherwise be multiple dwellings as a single dwelling if the multiple property:

- consists of a single self-contained unit, or such a unit together with or containing premises constructed or adapted for non-domestic purposes; *and*
- is occupied as more than one unit of separate living accommodation.[8]

This could apply, for example, to a property occupied by more than one household but where the residents share facilities such as kitchens or bathrooms, eg a group of bedsits or a hostel. In exercising this discretion the listing officer should have regard to all the circumstances of the case, including the extent, if any, to which the parts of the property separately occupied have been structurally altered. The listing officer's decision that a property with a number of different households consists of only one dwelling rather than several may have an impact not only on the single dwelling's valuation band but also on liability and entitlement to discounts or benefits.

What counts as a dwelling in Scotland?

In Scotland a 'dwelling' means any lands and heritages:

- which consist of one or more dwelling-houses with any garden, yard, garage, outhouse or pertinent belonging to and occupied with such dwelling-house or dwelling-houses; *and*
- which would, but for the fact that it is a dwelling, be entered separately in the valuation roll.[9]

The valuation roll is now limited to recording the details of non-domestic and part residential subjects.

The Scottish dwelling includes:

- the residential part of part residential subjects; *and*
- that part of any premises which has been apportioned, as at 1 April 1989, as a dwelling house.

It includes caravans but only if they are someone's sole or main residence (Chapter 6). The term 'caravan' has the same meaning as it has in Part I of the Caravan Sites and Control of Development Act 1960.

Property that counts as a dwelling

Certain types of property are explicitly included in or excluded from the Scottish definition of a dwelling. The following properties are specifically included in the definition of a dwelling:[10]

- a garage, car-port or car parking stance wholly or mainly used by private motor vehicles;[11]
- certain private storage premises used wholly or mainly for the storage of articles of domestic use (including cycles and other similar vehicles);[12]
- certain bed and breakfast accommodation;
- student halls;
- armed forces accommodation owned by the Ministry of Defence which are, or are likely to be, the sole or main residence of at least one member of the armed forces;
- school boarding accommodation;
- any part of a hostel, nursing home, private hospital or residential care home as defined for the purpose of a discount (Chapter 8) which are not used wholly or mainly as the sole or main residence of a person employed there.

While the above count as dwellings some of them are exempt from the tax (Chapter 5).[13] The definition of the accommodation described in the last point is the same as for disregards for council tax discount purposes (Chapter 8).

Excluded property

Certain properties are specifically excluded from the Scottish definition of a dwelling and are subject to non-domestic rates. The properties in question are:

- certain huts, sheds and bothies which are no one's sole or main residence;
- self-catering holiday accommodation which is no one's sole or main residence;

- women's refuges;[14] *and*
- timeshare accommodation.[15]

Scotland: part residential property

In Scotland lands and heritages which are part residential and part non-residential should be shown as such on the valuation roll.[16] An apportionment note on the roll indicates the net annual value and the rateable value based on the residential and non-residential use made of the property. Women's refuges and property defined as a hostel, nursing home, private hospital or residential care home for the purpose of a discount (Chapter 8) are specifically excluded from the definition of part residential subject.[17]

When does a new or altered building count as a new dwelling?

A new dwelling may come about as the result of either building or the structural alteration of an existing property. Authorities must identify new dwellings and refer them to the valuation officer or local assessor. Planning records and building control records are often used for this purpose. A new dwelling is considered to come into existence for council tax purposes from the day it is completed or the completion date contained on a completion notice if earlier.[18] It may however be exempt from the tax for a period (Chapter 5). Where the new dwelling is brought about by the structural alteration of a building the former dwelling or dwellings are considered to have ceased to exist on the completion date.

Completion notices

In England and Wales the authority, and in Scotland the local assessor may serve a completion notice on the owner of a building which has been completed or which can reasonably be expected to be completed within three months. This notice proposes a completion day for the building. The building becomes a dwelling for council tax purposes from the completion date.

The proposed completion day becomes the actual completion day unless an aggrieved person appeals. Prior to the outcome of the appeal the proposed completion day is treated as the actual completion day.

Appeals against completion notices

While any disagreement over the date on a completion notice may be raised with the authority in England and Wales or the assessor in Scotland, appeals must be made within particularly short time periods (Chapter 13). In England and Wales appeals should be made directly to the valuation tribunal within four weeks of the notice being sent. The president of the tribunal may, however, allow an out-of-time appeal where the aggrieved person has failed to meet this time limit for reasons beyond her/his control. In Scotland an appeal must be lodged with the valuation appeal committee within 21 days of receipt of the completion notice.[19] This is done by writing an appeal letter to the assessor stating the grounds of the appeal and enclosing a copy of the completion notice.

How is an appeal made against the valuation officer's or assessor's decision on a property?

In England and Wales it is the valuation officer (p17), and in Scotland the local assessor (p18), who decides in the first instance whether or not a property is a dwelling.

A proposal can be made at any time to the listing officer or local assessor if it is thought that a property should be included in or excluded from the valuation list.[20] For example if it is thought that accommodation should not be shown because it is not separate, self-contained accommodation. A proposal on this subject is made in the same way as a proposal to change the valuation band of a property (Chapter 3). Further appeals to a valuation tribunal in England and Wales or valuation appeal committee in Scotland are described in detail in Chapter 13.

CHAPTER THREE

Valuation

This chapter explains:

- who is responsible for council tax valuations;
- the valuation officer's or assessor's powers;
- how dwellings are valued;
- the nature and content of the valuation list;
- the public's right of access to the list; *and*
- how a dwelling's valuation band may be altered.

Who is responsible for valuations?

England and Wales

In England and Wales the initial and continuing valuation of dwellings for council tax purposes is carried out by the Valuation Office Agency (VOA) which is part of the Inland Revenue. A listing officer at the VOA has been appointed for each billing authority by the Inland Revenue Commissioners. The listing officer has various duties in relation to the compilation and maintenance of the valuation list. S/he is independent of the authority and paid for out of money provided by Parliament.[1] The term 'valuation officer' refers to any listing officer and any other officer appointed by the Commissioners to carry out any of their functions.[2] The valuation officer is based at the local office of the VOA.

Complaints procedures

The manner in which appeals may be made against the decision of a local valuation office is described later in this chapter and in Chapter 13. Complaints about the poor performance (as opposed to the decisions) of any local valuation office, however, should in the first instance be made to the office concerned. Where a satisfactory response to a complaint is not obtained a further complaint may be made to the relevant regional director of the VOA, or to a member of parliament, or (through an MP) to the Parliamentary Commissioner for Administration. People who are not satisfied with the regional director's response also have the option of putting their case to the Revenue Adjudicator. The Adjudicator should review all the facts and aim to reach a decision as speedily as possible. The VOA will normally accept the Adjudicator's decision unless there are very exceptional circumstances. Anyone who wishes to refer a complaint to the Revenue Adjudicator's Office may do so in writing or by telephone. The address is: Revenue Adjudicator's Office, 3rd Floor, Haymarket House, 28 Haymarket, London SW1Y 4SP. The telephone number is: 071 930 2292, fax: 071 930 2298.

Scotland

In Scotland the local assessor, and any depute assessor, for each regional and islands council decides which valuation band should apply to each dwelling in the area.[3] The assessor must comply with any directions regarding valuation given by the Inland Revenue Commissioners.[4] The assessor is paid for by the regional or islands council with assistance from central government.[5]

Appointees

In England and Wales the Commissioners, and in Scotland the assessor have also been empowered to appoint other people, such as private surveyors, to carry out valuations.[6] The Commissioners and the assessor are able to supply these appointees with relevant information obtained under their various powers.[7] If the person assisting with the valuation discloses that information, for reasons other than valuation purposes, s/he may be imprisoned for up to two years and/or fined on conviction or indictment. They may be imprisoned for up to six months and/or fined on summary conviction.[8]

What powers does the valuation officer or assessor have?

The valuation officer and assessor have powers:

- to enter dwellings; *and*
- to acquire information from a past or present owner, occupier, the authority and certain other people.

Powers of entry

A valuation officer and any assistant with written authorisation, and in Scotland the local assessor or depute assessor may enter, survey and value a dwelling.[9] This should only happen, however, where at least three clear days' notice has been given in writing. The three-day period excludes weekends and public holidays. Normally the official concerned should try and arrange a suitable time for access to the dwelling. Someone who intentionally delays or obstructs the official may be liable on summary conviction to a fine not exceeding level 2 on the standard scale.[10]

The owner's and occupier's obligation to supply information

The valuation officer and the local assessor may also require the present or past owner or occupier of a dwelling to supply information if it would be of assistance in carrying out the valuation.[11] If the information is in the owner's or occupier's possession or control it should be supplied within 21 days of a written notice being served. Failure to comply with this requirement, without reasonable excuse, may result in a fine up to scale 2 on the standard scale.[12]

A current or past owner or occupier who:

• makes a statement which is known to be false on a relevant point; *or*
• recklessly makes a statement which is false on a relevant point,

is liable on summary conviction to imprisonment for up to three months and/or a fine up to level 3 on the standard scale.[13]

The authority's obligation to provide information

The valuation officer and assessor may require the authority to supply information concerning a property so long as it is reasonably believed that the information will assist in carrying out the appropriate functions. Additionally if any information comes to the notice of an authority which it considers would assist the listing officer or assessor in her/his duties it should provide that information.[14] In practice it is the authority's task to identify new dwellings and refer existing ones that have been altered. Authorities may use, for example, planning records, building control reports and information about searches made by prospective purchasers of its land charges register to help identify appropriate cases to refer.

Right to use other sources of information

Certain other individuals and organisations, such as the community charge registration officer and in the Scottish context the district council, Scottish Homes and a new town development corporation must also supply requested information.[15] A valuation officer or assessor may also take into account any other information available from other sources.

How are dwellings valued?

Each dwelling is valued on the basis of what it might have reasonably been expected to realise in the open market, subject to certain valuation assumptions, if sold on 1 April 1991 by a willing seller.[16] The use of the same date for all valuations means that existing dwellings do not have to be adjusted for changes in prices through time. A new dwelling in September 1995 will be valued on the basis of its open market value as if it had been sold on 1 April 1991.

Many people consider this method of valuation unfair as they have seen the value of their homes fall since April 1991. The government's argument is that the purpose of the valuation for council tax purposes is to band dwellings according to their relative worth and for no other purpose. Consequently if there is a general change in property values this may well have affected all dwellings in a similar fashion. In reality, however, different types of dwelling may have different changes in price.

The valuation assumptions

To place all valuations on a common basis they are not only assessed on the basis of their market value as at 1 April 1991 but also on the basis of certain 'valuation assumptions'.[17] These assumptions are identified in Exhibit 3.1. Those which apply only to the valuation of dwellings in England and Wales or in Scotland are identified.

Fixtures for a disabled person

Fixtures are items in a dwelling which are permanently attached to it such as a sink, lavatory or lift. The value of fixtures should be ignored in the valuation if:

- they are designed to make the dwelling suitable for use by a physically disabled person; *and*
- they add to the dwelling's value.[18]

In other words the dwelling is valued on the basis that those fixtures are not present. There is no requirement that a physically disabled person actually lives in the dwelling. Such fixtures may have been taken into account during the valuation process. If this is the case the listing officer or local assessor should be advised of this possible oversight. In addition to the above there is a separate disability reduction scheme for people with disabilities. This is described in Chapter 7.

Exhibit 3.1 Valuation assumptions

- The sale was with vacant possession.
- That in England and Wales a house was sold freehold and a flat (ie part of a building divided horizontally to provide living units) was sold on a lease for 99 years at a nominal rent.
- The English or Welsh dwelling was sold free from any rentcharge (ie rare rental payments on freehold land usually associated with covenants) or other incumbrance.
- That the Scottish dwelling was sold free from any heritable security (ie any mortgage is paid off).
- The size, layout and character of the dwelling, and the physical state of its locality, were the same as on the day the valuation was made.
- The dwelling is in reasonable repair.
- Any common parts that a purchaser would have to contribute towards the upkeep of, such as an entrance or hallway shared with another dwelling, are in reasonable repair taking into account the age and character of the dwelling and its locality.
- Fixtures designed for a physically disabled person that increase the value of the dwelling are ignored.
- The use of the dwelling is permanently restricted to use as a private dwelling.
- The dwelling had no development value other than that attributable to any development for which no planning permission is required.

Valuation of dwellings with mixed domestic and business use

In England and Wales properties which include both a domestic and non-domestic component (known as a composite hereditament) are valued on the basis of the proportion of the open market value which might reasonably be attributed to the domestic use of the property. The valuation is based on the same rules and assumptions as outlined above except that the assumption that the property is permanently restricted to use as a private dwelling is ignored.[19]

Scottish farmhouses, crofts and fish farms

In Scotland dwellings such as farmhouses or cottages and croft houses connected with agriculture and dwellings connected with fish farms are valued on the basis that their availability is restricted to being used in that way. This lowers the valuation for such dwellings and may lower the valuation bands they are allocated to.[20]

Proposals and appeals on valuations

The use of the above assumptions means that a dwelling's valuation band may not reflect its actual sale price in 1991. For example if a dwelling was sold in April 1991 but in a poor state of repair or with sitting tenants then it may in reality have realised significantly less by way of sale price than its council tax banding would suggest. Consequently the selling price of such a dwelling would not be useful evidence to support a proposal to alter the valuation of a dwelling on the valuation list or at a valuation tribunal or valuation appeal committee hearing. To be successful any proposal for an alteration of a dwelling's banding or an appeal on the subject must be made on the basis of the assumptions described above.

How have valuation lists been compiled and maintained?

The listing officer or assessor was responsible for the compilation of each authority's valuation list. He or she is also responsible for its maintenance.[21]

Compilation of the list

To ensure the effective implementation of the council tax, the listing officer or assessor had a duty to supply the authority with copies of the proposed list on a number of dates prior to 1 April 1993. In most cases council tax bills have been based on the information contained in the advance list supplied in November 1992 or a later draft list supplied in February 1993. The actual valuation list was compiled on 1 April 1993 and came into force on that day. Prior to its compilation the listing officer or assessor should have taken such steps as were reasonably practicable in the time available to ensure that the list was accurate.[22] As soon as reasonably practicable after its compilation a copy should have been sent to the authority. The authority should have deposited it at its principal office.[23] While the public has rights of access to the valuation list (see below) the authority does not have the same obligation to advertise its availability, as it did with the last copy of the proposed list it received prior to 1 April 1993.

Maintenance of the list

The listing officer or assessor must maintain the list for so long as is necessary for the purposes of the council tax.[24] The listing officer or assessor notifies the authority on a regular basis of any alterations to the compiled list to take account of new dwellings, demolitions, successful appeals and other material changes. A snapshot of the valuation list is also provided on a periodic basis. For the purpose of determining for any day which valuation band is applicable to a dwelling, the state of affairs at the end of the day is assumed to have existed throughout that day.[25]

What does the valuation list show?

A valuation list must show the items identified in Exhibit 3.2.[26] Certain items only appear on a valuation list in England and Wales, others relate to Scotland. These are indicated in the Exhibit. The list does not contain any personal information. The omission from a list of any matter required to be included in it does not make it invalid.[27]

Exhibit 3.2   The contents of a valuation list

- Each dwelling in the authority's area.
- Each dwelling's valuation band.
- A reference number for each dwelling.
- A marker indicating properties with mixed domestic and non-domestic use (a composite hereditament) (England and Wales only).
- The effective date where there has been an alteration.
- An indicator showing that an alteration has been made following an order of a valuation tribunal or the High Court or in Scotland a valuation appeal committee or the Court of Session.
- Notes indicating that a dwelling is a private garage, domestic storage premises, etc. (Scotland only).

When may members of the public see the list?

While the banding of the liable person's dwelling is indicated on the council tax bill or notification relating to an exempt dwelling, everybody has the right to inspect the valuation list. Access to this information must be provided free of charge and at a reasonable time and place.[28]

The valuation list may be in whatever form the authority, listing officer or assessor consider appropriate, eg documentary, microfiche, computer visual display, etc. Members of the public may make copies or transcripts of the list, or parts of the list. Alternatively the authority, the listing officer or the assessor are required to supply a copy if requested to do so but a reasonable charge may be made for this service. The authority cannot, however, sell copies of the list, for example to direct mail companies. If someone is intentionally obstructed from exercising her/his rights in relation to the valuation list the person responsible for the obstruction may be liable on summary conviction to a fine not exceeding level 2 on the standard scale.[29]

When can a valuation list be altered?

The government does not have any plans to carry out a revaluation of all dwellings in the future. The valuation list, including an individual dwelling's valuation band, may only be altered:

- by the listing officer or the assessor;
- following receipt of a proposal from an interested party or the authority; *or*
- following a successful appeal.

Exhibit 3.3 indicates the circumstances in which a dwelling's valuation band may be altered.[30]

Most of the items in Exhibit 3.3 are self-explanatory but the concept of a material change in the dwelling's value is worth examining in greater detail.

A material increase in the dwelling's value

A material increase in the value of a dwelling means any increase which is caused (in whole or in part) by any:

- building;
- engineering; *or*
- other operation carried out in relation to the dwelling.[31]

This would apply to building or other works which either increase the size of the property or add to its market value. But the material increase only has an impact on the dwelling's valuation once the dwelling (or any part of it) has been sold. In England and Wales this also applies where the dwelling is let on a lease for a term of seven years or more.

Exhibit 3.3   Circumstances in which a valuation band may be altered

- The listing officer or assessor is satisfied that the valuation band is incorrect due, for example, to a clerical error.
- The listing officer or assessor is satisfied that the dwelling would have been allocated to a different valuation band if the valuation had been carried out correctly.
- There has been a material increase in the value of the dwelling since it was placed on the list and all or part of it has been sold or additionally in England and Wales let on a lease for a term of seven years or more.
- There has been a material reduction in the value of the dwelling.
- Part of a property starts to be used, or is no longer used, for business purposes or the balance between business and domestic use changes.
- There has been a successful appeal against the valuation band shown on the list.

Example

The owner adds a double storey extension to his house in the summer of 1993. While it is hoped that the value of the property has increased as a result of the extension it has no impact on the dwelling's valuation band for council tax purposes. It is only when the house is sold in the winter of 1996 that the dwelling should be revalued on the basis of its April 1991 market value and, if appropriate, allocated to a new valuation band.

What counts as a material reduction?

A material reduction in the value of a dwelling should lead to an immediate revaluation. This, if significant enough, will also lead to an immediate rebanding of the dwelling. This only applies, however, if the reduction is caused (in whole or in part) by:

- the demolition (but not partial demolition during other building or engineering work) of any part of the dwelling;
- any change in the physical state of the dwelling's locality; *or*
- any adaptation of the dwelling to make it suitable for use by a physically disabled person.[32]

Changes in the physical state of a dwelling's locality give the greatest scope for proposals to change a dwelling's valuation band.

Such changes include, for example, a change in the character of the dwelling's immediate environment brought about as the result of a road widening scheme, the deterioration of surrounding property or a change in the use of nearby business premises.

Where fixtures such as bars or concrete ramps designed to make the dwelling suitable for use by a physically disabled person reduce the value of the dwelling, they should be taken into account in the valuation process and therefore reflected in its banding. There is no requirement that a physically disabled person actually lives in the dwelling. This provision is in addition to the disability reduction scheme described in Chapter 7.

How is a dwelling revalued?

When one of the conditions for the potential alteration of a dwelling's valuation band exists a revaluation should occur. The valuation should be made on the basis of the rules and assumptions already described which means that its value, taking account of its current state, is based on what it would have sold for on the open market by a willing vendor on 1 April 1991.[33] If the change in value is only small it may not be enough to move a dwelling from one valuation band to another.

How is an alteration to the list obtained?

Where a list is inaccurate, for example because a dwelling's valuation band does not correctly reflect its valuation (carried out as described above) a proposal may be made to the listing officer or assessor for an alteration to the list. In many instances there are time limits for the making of proposals – see below. The making of a proposal is also a first and obligatory stage in the appeal process (Chapter 13).

People who can make a proposal

An interested person can make a proposal. An interested person on any particular day is:

- the owner of the dwelling;
- anyone who is liable (either solely or jointly) to pay the tax on the dwelling; *and*
- in the case of an exempt dwelling (Chapter 5), or a dwelling on which the council tax has been set at nil, the person who would otherwise be liable to pay the tax.[34]

In England and Wales the authority can also make a proposal to the listing officer.[35]

What are the time limits for making proposals?

The ability to make proposals in certain circumstances is subject to time limits.

Proposals regarding a valuation band on the original list

If it is thought that an incorrect valuation band has been applied to a dwelling that was on the valuation list compiled on 1 April 1993 the proposal must be made by 30 November 1993.[36]

In Scotland a proposal may also be made within six months of the issue of the first bill ('demand notice') showing the final valuation band for the dwelling if the banding changed between the draft list of 1 December 1992 and the actual list of 1 April 1993.[37] Also in Scotland the proposal may be made within six months of receiving notification from the authority that the dwelling is considered exempt from 1 April 1993.[38]

Banding proposals made by a new resident/owner or regarding a new property

A proposal may be made within a six-month period where:

• someone first becomes liable for the council tax on a particular dwelling; *or*
• the dwelling, for example a new home, is first shown on the valuation list after 1 April 1993.[39]

Such a proposal cannot be made, however, where:

• it is based on the same facts as have already been considered and determined by an appeal body; *or*
• the new taxpayer is a company which is a subsidiary of the immediately preceding taxpayer; *or*
• the immediately preceding taxpayer is a company which is a subsidiary of the new taxpayer; *or*
• both the new and the immediately preceding taxpayers are companies which are subsidiaries of the same company; *or*
• the change of taxpayer has occurred solely by reason of the formation of a new partnership in relation to which any of the partners was a partner in the previous partnership.[40]

Appeal decisions relating to a comparable dwelling

An appeal may be made within six months of an appeal decision on a comparable dwelling which gives reasonable grounds for contending that the valuation band for the dwelling in question should be changed.[41]

Proposals regarding an alteration to the list

Where the listing officer or the assessor has altered the list in respect of a dwelling, a proposal can be made within six months from the service of the notice of the alteration.[42]

Other proposals

A proposal may be made at any time where:

- a property should be excluded from, or included in, the valuation list;[43]
- there has been a material increase in the dwelling and a relevant transaction;
- there has been a material reduction in the value of a dwelling;
- part of a property starts to be used, or is no longer used, for business use or the balance between business and domestic use changes.[44]

How should a proposal be made?

The proposal is made by writing to the listing officer at the local office of the Valuation Office Agency (the address should be on the council tax bill and in the local telephone book) or the local assessor.[45] Standard forms and explanatory notes are available from these offices to assist those wishing to make proposals. The completed form or alternatively a letter should contain all relevant information including:

- the name and address of the proposer;
- the capacity in which the proposal is made, such as that of liable person or as the owner of the dwelling;
- the dwelling to which it relates;
- the way in which it is proposed the list should be altered and the date; *and*
- the reasons for believing the list to be inaccurate, the relevant facts, any evidence supporting those facts and any relevant dates such as the date someone first became the liable person or the date a material reduction in the dwelling occurred.[46]

Can a proposal relate to more than one dwelling?

Normally a proposal may only deal with one dwelling. In England and Wales, however, there are explicit provisions for a proposal to deal with more than one dwelling where:

- the proposer makes the proposal in the same capacity, ie owner, and each of the dwellings is within the same building or curtilage as the other or others; *or*
- it arises because a property is shown as a dwelling when it should not be or should be a number of dwellings.[47]

Service of the proposal

The proposal should be addressed to the listing officer or assessor for the relevant area and delivered or sent by post to the appropriate address.[48] To be on the safe side it is sensible to obtain some proof of postage, eg registered mail or, if delivered by hand a receipt. A copy of the proposal should also be kept.

Acknowledging receipt of the proposal

In England and Wales the listing officer should write acknowledging receipt of the proposal within 28 days unless it is considered to be invalid. In keeping with Citizens' Charter principles the VOA has set standards of service for handling appeals. The local valuation office's objective is to acknowledge receipt of proposals within 14 days (DoE press release, 29 June 1993). The acknowledgement should also include details of the procedures that will be followed.[49]

In Scotland the assessor should in all cases write acknowledging receipt of the proposal within 14 days. Again the acknowledgement letter should include details of the procedures that will be followed.[50]

Provision for joint proposals in Scotland

In Scotland where a proposal has been made other interested persons may write to the assessor indicating that they wish to support the proposal.[51] As long as the proposal has not been withdrawn or referred to the local valuation appeal panel the original proposal should then be treated as a joint proposal.

When is a proposal considered invalid?

Different procedures operate in relation to invalid proposals in England and Wales and in Scotland. The English and Welsh procedures are considered first then those that apply in Scotland. The failure by the listing officer or assessor to identify an invalid proposal at this stage does not stop that point being raised at an appeal hearing.[52]

Invalid proposals: England and Wales

In England and Wales if the listing officer considers that the proposal is invalid an 'invalidity notice' is sent to the proposer. This should be done within four weeks of receipt of the proposal. This notice gives:

- the reasons why the proposal is considered invalid; *and*
- the procedure to be followed.[53]

The listing officer may at any time withdraw an invalidity notice by informing the proposer of that fact in writing.

Unless an invalidity notice has been withdrawn the proposer may:

- make a further proposal – but only once and only if the original proposal was made within the appropriate time limit; *or*
- appeal to the valuation tribunal against the invalidity notice by writing to the listing officer disagreeing with the invalidity notice. Legally the proposer's letter is called a 'notice of disagreement'.[54]

In the latter circumstances, unless the listing officer withdraws the invalidity notice within four weeks of receipt of the notice of disagreement, the matter goes on to the relevant valuation tribunal. The listing officer should write to the clerk of the tribunal giving:

- the relevant entry in the list (if any);
- the grounds on which the proposal was made; *and*
- the listing officer's reasons for considering the proposal invalid.[55]

Tribunal hearings are described in Chapter 13. Action on the original proposal is suspended until either the listing officer withdraws the invalidity notice or the tribunal or High Court reaches a decision on the validity of the proposal.

Invalid proposals: Scotland

In Scotland a distinction is drawn between proposals that are considered invalid:

- because the proposer is not an appropriate person to make such a proposal or because it is out of time; *or*
- because the proposal does not include the required information.[56]

In both instances the assessor must write to the proposer within six weeks of receipt of the proposal. In the first instance the letter must give reasons for the decision and describe the proposer's right to appeal in writing to the assessor within four weeks. If no such appeal is made the matter will have ended. In the second instance the letter must again give reasons for the decision but should also identify the information that needs to be supplied. The proposer may either:

- supply the information in which case this should be done within four weeks; *or*
- appeal in writing to the assessor – again within four weeks.

If the information is not supplied or an appeal is not made within the four-week period then the assessor treats the proposal as invalidly made and that is the end of the matter.

If an appeal is made in either case but the assessor still considers the appeal invalid s/he should inform the secretary of the local valuation appeal panel in writing within four weeks that an appeal has been made. Details of the proposal and the assessor's reason for considering the proposal invalid should also be given.[57]

What happens after a valid proposal has been made?

The procedures relating to valid proposals again differ between England and Wales, and Scotland. The English and Welsh procedures are considered first and then those that apply in Scotland.

England and Wales

Within six weeks of receiving a valid proposal the listing officer should send a copy of it to anyone else who appears to be liable for the tax on the dwelling. Copies should also be sent to the authority where it has informed the listing officer in writing that it wishes to receive a copy of a class or classes of proposal, and the proposal falls within such a class. Each copy should be accompanied by a statement of the procedures to be followed.[58]

Following the receipt of a valid proposal one of four things may happen:

- the listing officer may agree to the proposal;
- all interested parties may agree to an alternative alteration to the list;
- an appeal may be made to the valuation tribunal; *or*
- the proposal may be withdrawn.

The listing officer agrees to the proposal

Where the listing officer agrees to the proposal the proposer, and the liable person (if different), should be notified that the valuation list will be altered accordingly. The valuation list should be altered within six weeks of the date of the letter.[59]

Agreeing to a different alteration

It is possible for the listing officer and the proposer to agree an alteration to the list that is different from that proposed. To take effect this requires the agreement of all interested parties. For instance, if the proposer is different from the liable person such an agreement also requires the signature of the liable person (or one of the jointly liable persons) at the time of the agreement. Additionally if someone else was liable at the time the proposal was made and the listing officer is able to ascertain their whereabouts the former liable person or one of the former jointly liable persons must also agree. Where such an agreement is reached the listing officer should alter the valuation list within six weeks of the date of the agreement. The original proposal is treated as withdrawn.[60]

Appeal to the valuation tribunal

Within six months of receipt of the proposal by the listing officer it must be referred as an appeal to the relevant valuation tribunal if:

- the listing officer is of the opinion that a proposal is incorrect;
- the proposal is not withdrawn; *and*
- there is no agreement as to an alternative alteration.[61]

There is nothing to stop the listing officer referring the matter to a valuation tribunal sooner if no progress is being made on a possible agreement. The VOA's stated intention is that 'council tax payers should have their appeals settled as quickly and efficiently as possible'. In addition it considers that 'appropriate priority should be given to identified cases of hardship'. (DoE press release, 29 June 1993.)

The listing officer should send the clerk of the tribunal a statement detailing:

- the entry in the list (if any) which is proposed to be altered;
- the date of receipt of the proposal by the listing officer;
- the names and addresses (where known to the listing officer) of all persons whose agreement is required; *and*
- the grounds on which the proposal was made.[62]

Appeals are described in Chapter 13.

Withdrawing the proposal

The proposer may withdraw the proposal at any time by writing to the listing officer.[63] A proposal may not be withdrawn, however, where the proposer made it as a liable person and is no longer a liable person in respect of the dwelling concerned, unless the liable person at the date of the withdrawal agrees in writing. In the case of joint liability the agreement of only one of the liable persons is required.[64]

Where someone else has an interest in the proposal, ie an owner or a liable person, and has written to inform the listing officer of that interest within three months of the listing officer receiving the proposal, that other person must be notified of its withdrawal. If that other person writes back to the listing officer within six weeks of receipt of the letter advising of the withdrawal and says that s/he is aggrieved by its withdrawal they may take it over. This is only possible, however, if they were an interested person on the date the original proposal was made. Any resulting alteration takes effect from the day it would have done had there been no withdrawal of the proposal.

Scotland

In Scotland following the receipt of a valid proposal one of three things may happen:

● the assessor may agree to the proposal;
● an appeal may be made to the local valuation appeal panel; *or*
● the proposal may be withdrawn.

Alteration agreed by the assessor

Where the assessor thinks the proposal is well founded the proposer and any joint proposer should be advised of that in a letter. The list should be altered within six weeks of the date of that letter.[65]

Appeal to the local valuation appeal panel

Where the assessor thinks that the proposal is not well-founded, and it is not withdrawn, s/he should refer the disagreement to the local valuation appeal panel. This should be done within six months from the day the assessor received the proposal.[66]

Where the assessor has previously issued an invalidity notice on the grounds that:

- the proposer is not an appropriate person to make the proposal or the proposal is out of time, the six-month period starts from the day the assessor withdrew the notice or the proposer won the appeal against the notice;
- the proposal does not include the required information the six-month period starts from the day that all the relevant information was supplied or the day the proposer won the appeal against the notice.[67]

A proposal may be adopted by another interested person if the original proposer seeks to withdraw it. In such cases the six-month period starts from the date that other person informed the assessor of the wish to adopt the proposal.[68]

The appeal is initiated by the assessor writing to the secretary of the valuation panel advising of the appeal. The following information should also be included:

- the proposed alteration of the list;
- the date the proposal was received;
- the name and address of the proposer; *and*
- the grounds on which the proposal was made.[69]

Appeals are described in Chapter 13.

Withdrawing the proposal

The proposal may be withdrawn at any time if the proposer or proposers write to the assessor.[70] If none of the proposers are currently liable for the tax on the dwelling the assessor must write to at least one currently liable person telling them about the proposed withdrawal. An interested person has six weeks from the date of the letter to advise the assessor of a wish to adopt the proposal. From that date it is then treated as made by that person.

What notification should the listing officer or assessor provide?

Within six weeks of altering the list the listing officer or assessor should write to the authority stating the effect of the alteration. The authority should alter its copy of the valuation list as soon as is reasonably practicable.[71]

England and Wales

In England and Wales the listing officer should also write to the person who is currently liable for the tax on the dwelling advising them of the effect of the alteration and the process by which a proposal and appeal may be made.[72] This obligation to notify does not apply however in relation to alterations effected solely for the purpose of correcting a clerical error, or for reflecting:

- a decision of the listing officer that a proposal is well-founded;
- an agreed alternative alteration; *or*
- a change in the address of the dwelling concerned; *or*
- a change in the area of the billing authority; *or*
- the decision of a valuation tribunal or the High Court in relation to the dwelling concerned.

The listing officer should take such steps as are reasonably practicable to ensure that the letter to the liable person goes out no later than the letter to the authority.[73]

Scotland

In Scotland the assessor must also notify someone liable for the tax on the dwelling within six weeks of the alteration being made. Where the alteration involves the addition of the dwelling to the list the owner must also be notified within six weeks of the alteration.

Additionally the assessor must also notify someone liable for the tax on the dwelling within six weeks of the alteration being made where:

- an alteration has been agreed to but the proposer is not a liable person at the time of the alteration; *or*
- an appeal decision has led to the alteration of the list but none of the parties to the appeal is a liable person on the date of the alteration.[74]

The above notification should include a statement about the process by which a proposal may be made. The assessor should take such steps as are reasonably practicable to ensure that the above letters go out no later than the letter to the authority.[75]

When may members of the public see information about proposals and appeals?

Any member of the public may, at a reasonable time and without making payment, inspect any proposal or appeal made in relation to the current list, or any list in force within the preceding five years.[76] Copies of that material may be made or alternatively the listing officer or assessor must provide copies of the relevant information. A reasonable charge may be made for this service. It is an offence for the person responsible for the material, without reasonable excuse:

- to intentionally obstruct someone from obtaining access to the material; *or*
- to refuse to supply a copy of the relevant material.

On summary conviction s/he may be fined up to level 2 on the standard scale.

CHAPTER FOUR

The amount of tax

This chapter explains:

- the valuation bands that apply in England, Scotland and Wales;
- the relationship between a dwelling's valuation band and the amount of tax, and in Scotland council water charge, payable; *and*
- the ways in which the amount of tax payable may be reduced.

What are the valuation bands?

Each year authorities must set a council tax to help pay for their expenditure and that of related bodies. The authority must publish the amounts of its council tax within 21 days of setting them in at least one local newspaper. Failure to do so however does not invalidate the amounts.[1] The council tax and Scottish water charge is set on the basis that different amounts are payable in respect of dwellings in the different valuation bands. Different valuation bands apply in England,[2] Scotland[3] and Wales[4] (Exhibits 4.1–4.3).

Exhibit 4.1 The valuation bands in England			
Valuation band	*Range of values*		
A	Up to £40,000		
B	Over £40,000	and up to	£52,000
C	Over £52,000	and up to	£68,000
D	Over £68,000	and up to	£88,000
E	Over £88,000	and up to	£120,000
F	Over £120,000	and up to	£160,000
G	Over £160,000	and up to	£320,000
H	Over £320,000		

Exhibit 4.2   The valuation bands in Scotland

Valuation band	Range of values		
A	Up to £27,000		
B	Over £27,000	and up to	£35,000
C	Over £35,000	and up to	£45,000
D	Over £45,000	and up to	£58,000
E	Over £58,000	and up to	£80,000
F	Over £80,000	and up to	£106,000
G	Over £106,000	and up to	£212,000
H	Over £212,000		

Exhibit 4.3   The valuation bands in Wales

Valuation band	Range of values		
A	Up to £30,000		
B	Over £30,000	and up to	£39,000
C	Over £39,000	and up to	£51,000
D	Over £51,000	and up to	£66,000
E	Over £66,000	and up to	£90,000
F	Over £90,000	and up to	£120,000
G	Over £120,000	and up to	£240,000
H	Over £240,000		

How does the amount of tax payable vary between bands?

The council tax payable in any authority depends on the valuation band the dwelling has been placed in. The lower the value of the band the lower the bill. The amount of tax payable in respect of dwellings situated in the same area varies between valuation bands in the following proportions:[5]

$$6(A):7(B):8(C):9(D):11(E):13(F):15(G):18(H)$$

This means, for example, that the tax payable on a chargeable band H dwelling is three times more than a band A dwelling and double that of a band D dwelling. The authority has no discretion to vary bands or the relative proportion of tax paid within each band.

Daily liability

Liability to pay the tax arises on a daily basis. The situation at the end of the day is assumed to have existed throughout the day.[6] The amount payable for the day is the annual amount set by the authority for that year for the dwellings in the relevant valuation bands divided by the number of days in the financial year (ie 365/366).

How may the tax payable be reduced?

Individual dwellings

The amount payable in respect of a specific dwelling may be reduced by:

- an alteration to the dwelling's valuation band (Chapter 3);
- a fixed period, or indefinite, exemption (Chapter 5);
- a disability reduction (Chapter 7);
- a discount (Chapter 8);
- a transitional reduction (Chapter 9);
- council tax benefit (Chapter 10); *and*
- the adoption of certain payment arrangements which may offer a discount (Chapter 11).

Tax capping

The Local Government Finance Act 1992 provides powers for the appropriate Secretary of State to limit the amount of council tax set. The Secretary of State has power to designate authorities where:

- the budget requirement is considered excessive; *or*
- there is an excessive increase in that amount over the amount calculated for the previous year.[7]

Designation is by general principles, and a maximum for the amount concerned is specified. Authorities are able to challenge or accept the maximum. Consequential reductions in the amount of council tax for the area concerned have to be made.

Appeals

The decisions taken by the authority in setting the amount of tax payable in the year are not the subject of a normal appeal but may be the subject of a judicial review.[8]

CHAPTER FIVE

Exempt dwellings

This chapter explains:

- which dwellings are exempt from the council tax, and in Scotland the council water charge;
- how an authority decides which dwellings are exempt;
- the information that must be supplied by, and to, the authority in relation to exempt dwellings; *and*
- how an appeal is made against the authority's refusal to grant an exemption.

The council tax, and in Scotland the council water charge, is only payable in respect of chargeable dwellings. In England, Wales and Scotland the appropriate Secretary of State has specified that certain classes of dwelling are exempt from the council tax.[1] No council tax is payable on a dwelling on any day it falls into an exempt category. The authority, not the listing officer or local assessor, must take steps each year to ascertain which dwellings in its area are exempt. For the purpose of determining for any day whether the dwelling is exempt the state of affairs at the end of the day is assumed to have existed throughout that day.[2]

Which dwellings are exempt in England and Wales?

Exhibit 5.1 summarises these classes for England and Wales. Exhibit 5.2 (p49) summarises these categories for Scotland.[3] Additional rules apply in both cases. These may be found in the text following the appropriate Exhibit and under the appropriate heading.

Vacant, unoccupied and occupied dwellings

In certain cases exemptions apply where the dwelling is vacant, in many cases where the dwelling is unoccupied and in some cases where the dwelling is occupied or unoccupied.

The term 'vacant' refers to a dwelling which is both unoccupied and substantially unfurnished.[4] The legislation contains no definition of 'substantially unfurnished' – the words therefore have their dictionary meaning. In practice many authorities regard a dwelling as 'substantially unfurnished' if in their opinion there are insufficient furnishings to enable someone to live in the dwelling. The legislation does define an unoccupied dwelling as one in which no one lives and an occupied dwelling as one in which at least one person lives.[5] There is, however, a significant distinction between occupying a home and being solely or mainly resident in it. While the same person may occupy two or more dwellings at any one time s/he can only be mainly resident in one of them. The authority must consider each case on its merits.

Exhibit 5.1   Exempt dwellings: England and Wales

Further conditions are described in the text

An unoccupied dwelling:
- which is substantially unfurnished and requires, or is undergoing, or has recently received major repairs or structural alterations to make it habitable;
- which belongs to a charity and which has been unoccupied for less than six months;
- which is substantially unfurnished for less than six months;
- which was previously the sole or main residence of someone in prison or certain other forms of detention;
- where someone has died;
- where occupation is prohibited by law;
- which is being kept for occupation by a minister of religion;
- which was previously the sole or main residence of someone in a hospital, nursing or residential care home, or certain hostels;
- which was previously the sole or main residence of someone who is receiving care in a place other than a hospital or a home;
- which was previously the sole or main residence of someone who is resident elsewhere providing personal care;
- which was previously the sole or main residence of a student resident elsewhere or a person who will become a student within six weeks of vacating the dwelling;
- which is in the possession of a mortgage lender;
- which is held by trustees in bankruptcy.

Other dwellings:
- student halls of residence;
- wholly occupied by students or school or college leavers;
- armed forces accommodation.

Vacant dwelling requiring or undergoing major repairs or alterations

A dwelling is exempt indefinitely if it is a vacant dwelling (ie unoccupied and substantially unfurnished) which:

- requires, or is undergoing, major repair works to make it habitable; or
- is undergoing structural alteration which has not been substantially completed.[6]

The vacant dwelling remains exempt for as long as it requires the major repair work or for as long as the works or alteration takes. Major repair works includes structural repair works.

Vacant dwelling which has been recently repaired or altered

A vacant dwelling remains exempt from the council tax for an additional period of up to six months from the day on which repair works were, or structural alteration was, substantially completed. In considering whether a dwelling has been vacant (ie unoccupied and substantially unfurnished) for any period, any one period, not exceeding six weeks, during which it was not vacant should be disregarded.[7]

Example

A landlord purchases a large, empty house with a view to converting it into two self-contained flats for rent. The alterations commence after one month and take 10 months to complete. The property is exempt for the first month because it is vacant. It is also exempt throughout the period when the alterations are being undertaken.

Unfortunately, the landlord is unable to let either of the two flats as soon as they are completed. He has purchased a job-lot of furniture and decides to put all of this into the ground-floor flat for the time being. The first-floor flat remains vacant.

On completion, the first-floor flat, being vacant, will continue to be exempt for a further period of up to six months. The ground-floor flat becomes chargeable as soon as works are completed because, although it is unoccupied, it is not vacant (ie not also substantially unfurnished).

Should the first-floor flat be let within six months of completion, however, the exemption will cease on the day it is first occupied by the new tenant. If there is a delay in the new tenant moving in, the exemption does not end on the day on which the tenancy comes into effect (since the dwelling is still vacant on that day) but on the day he or she actually takes up occupancy (provided the flat has not ceased to be vacant because he or she has moved in furniture beforehand and the maximum six-month time limit has not already expired in the meantime).

Unoccupied charitable dwelling

An unoccupied dwelling owned by a body established solely for charitable purposes is exempt for up to six months from the last day it was occupied. For this exemption to apply the charity must be the freeholder or hold the most inferior (ie shortest) leasehold interest for a term of six months or more. The dwelling may be furnished or unfurnished. The exemption only applies, however, if it was last occupied in furtherance of the objects of the charity. For the purpose of deciding the day on which the dwelling was last occupied any period of occupation of less than six weeks should be disregarded.[8] This exemption can be repeated each time the dwelling is unoccupied following a period of occupation of six weeks or more as long as the above conditions are met.

Unoccupied and substantially unfurnished dwelling

A vacant dwelling (one that is unoccupied; and substantially unfurnished) is exempt for up to six months.[9] This exemption can apply both to new and previously occupied dwellings. In considering whether a dwelling has been vacant for any period, any one period, not exceeding six weeks, during which it was not vacant is disregarded.

Dwelling unoccupied because owner in prison

An unoccupied dwelling is exempt indefinitely if the owner (ie the freeholder or the person with the most inferior (ie shortest) leasehold interest for a term of six months or more) is in prison or certain other forms of detention and s/he would be the sole or main resident of the dwelling but for the detention.[10] For the purpose of this exemption a person is considered detained if s/he would be regarded as such for the purpose of a council tax discount (Chapter 8).[11]

The dwelling is also exempt if the owner was previously the sole or main resident and previously detained but since the end of that detention has been in a hospital, residential care home, hostel, or other accommodation where care is provided or providing personal care to someone else.

Example

On leaving prison the former prisoner moves in with his elderly mother to provide care. In such circumstances the home owned by the former prisoner remains exempt.

Dwelling left unoccupied because the owner is in a hospital or home

An unoccupied dwelling is exempt indefinitely if it was previously the sole or main residence of an owner:

- who would be disregarded for the purpose of a council tax discount because s/he is a patient in hospital, residential care or nursing home or their Scottish equivalents as defined for discount purposes (Chapter 8); *and*
- since the dwelling was last occupied the owner has either been in that type of accommodation, in detention or receiving or providing care elsewhere.[12]

Dwelling left unoccupied because the owner is receiving care elsewhere

An unoccupied dwelling is exempt indefinitely if it was the sole or main residence of the owner (ie the freeholder or the leaseholder with the shortest lease of six months or more) who now has her/his sole or main residence in another place for the purpose of receiving personal care (but not a hospital, residential care home, nursing home, mental nursing home or certain hostels as described above).[13] The personal care must be required because of the owner's:

- old age;
- disablement;
- illness;
- past or present alcohol or drug dependence; *or*
- past or present mental disorder.

To qualify under this heading the owner must have been resident in such accommodation or detained, or in a hospital, nursing or residential care home (as described above) or resident somewhere else to provide care (as described below) since the dwelling last ceased to be her/his residence.

Dwelling left unoccupied because the owner is providing care elsewhere

An unoccupied dwelling is exempt indefinitely where it was previously the sole or main residence of an owner who is now solely or mainly resident elsewhere for the purpose of providing, or better providing, personal care to someone.[14] The owner is the freeholder or if there is one the leaseholder with the shortest lease of six months or more.

To qualify for this exemption the carer does not have to be disregarded for the purpose of a council tax discount. The person being cared for must, however, require the care due to her/his old age, disablement, illness, past or present alcohol or drug dependence or past or present mental disorder. In addition the owner-carer must have been absent from her/his own dwelling since it was last occupied either because s/he has been providing such care or because s/he has been under detention, in a hospital, nursing or residential care home (as described above).

Unoccupied dwelling where someone has died

Exemptions under this heading are limited to unoccupied dwellings where the only person who would be liable for the tax on the dwelling, but for this exemption, would be liable as the personal representative of a deceased person; and no grant of probate or of letters of administration has been made.[15] The exemption ends six months after a grant of probate or of letters of administration has been made.

Dwelling where occupation is prohibited

An unoccupied dwelling is exempt indefinitely where its occupation is prohibited by law.[16] It is also exempt where it is kept unoccupied by reason of action taken under powers conferred by, or under, any Act of Parliament, with a view to prohibiting its occupation or to acquiring it under a compulsory purchase order. If the dwelling is actually occupied, for example, by squatters then the dwelling is not exempt from the charge but it is the squatters who would normally be liable to pay the tax (Chapter 6).

Unoccupied dwelling held for a minister of religion

An unoccupied dwelling, such as a vicarage, is exempt indefinitely if it is held for the purpose of being available for occupation by a minister of any religious denomination as a residence from which to perform the duties of her/his office.[17]

Unoccupied dwelling in the possession of a mortgage lender

An unoccupied dwelling is exempt indefinitely where a mortgagee (ie a mortgage lender such as a bank, building society or finance company) is in possession under the mortgage.[18] This would arise, for example, where the lender repossessed the property due to the purchaser's failure to keep up payments on a mortgage.

Armed forces accommodation

Dwellings that are occupied or unoccupied are exempt indefinitely if they are:

- owned by the Secretary of State for Defence; *and*
- held for the purposes of armed forces accommodation.[19]

This includes, for example, armed forces barracks and married quarters. Contributions in place of the council tax are paid by the Ministry of Defence to authorities. These contributions should broadly match the amount which otherwise would have been payable.[20]

Visiting forces accommodation

A dwelling is exempt indefinitely where at least one person who would be liable is a member of a visiting force (or their dependants) where they are neither British citizens nor ordinarily resident in the United Kingdom.[21]

Unoccupied dwelling held by trustee in bankruptcy

An unoccupied dwelling is exempt indefinitely where the liable owner would be a trustee in bankruptcy under the Bankruptcy Act 1914 or the Insolvency Act 1986.[22] A trustee in bankruptcy is the person appointed by a general meeting of a bankrupt person's creditors, or the court, whose duty it is to take over all the property of the bankrupt, sell the property for cash and distribute the resulting funds amongst the creditors.

Dwelling left unoccupied by student owner

An unoccupied dwelling is exempt indefinitely where it was last occupied as the sole or main residence of its owner who is now a student and s/he:

- has been a student since having been solely or mainly resident in the dwelling; *or*
- has become a student within six weeks of the day occupation of the dwelling as a sole or main residence ceased.[23]

Student has the same meaning as for council tax discount purposes (see p79). If there are joint owners of the unoccupied property then all of them must now be students and at least one of them must have been solely or mainly resident there on the last day it was occupied and the last one must have become a student within six weeks of the day it was last occupied as a sole or main residence.

Example

A single student is studying in London. He left his former home in Plymouth and came to London three weeks before his course was due to start in order to give himself time to find rented accommodation. His flat in Plymouth, which he owns, remains unoccupied apart from when he returns for short periods during college vacations.

The flat in Plymouth is exempt because it is unoccupied and the owner became a student within six weeks of last having been solely resident there. It remains exempt when the student returns in the vacations since, during these times, it is occupied but the sole resident is a student. If the student decided to let the flat in Plymouth to a tenant it would cease to be exempt because it would no longer be unoccupied. However, it would continue to be exempt if the new tenant was also a student.

If the student decided to remain in London after completing his course, his unoccupied flat in Plymouth would cease to be exempt from the day after the last day of the course. But if the flat was vacant (eg all the furniture had been moved, sold or put in store in order to enable the flat to be sold) then an exemption could continue for a further period of up to six months. However, this particular six-month period would run from the day he last occupied the flat (ignoring any periods of occupation of six weeks or less) and *not* from the day he ceased to be a student. This means, for example, that if he finished his course four months after last having occupied his flat then only a further two months' exemption would apply.

Student hall of residence

A dwelling is exempt indefinitely under this heading if it is a hall of residence provided predominantly for the accommodation of students (but not student nurses) who would be disregarded for the purpose of a discount (see p79).[24] To qualify for the exemption the hall must be either:

- owned or managed by prescribed educational institutions (Exhibit 8.2); or
- the subject of an agreement allowing such an institution to nominate the majority of the persons who are to occupy the accommodation.

A hall should be exempt even if some non-students (such as wardens, tutors or dependants) live in the hall. Any separate self-contained flat or house provided for a non-student such as a caretaker or other member of staff is not covered by this exemption. If a hall of residence is used for more than 140 days a year for commercial purposes, such as conferences, it may be subject to non-domestic rates for that period.

Dwelling wholly occupied by students

To be exempt under this heading the dwelling must be either:

- occupied by one or more residents all of whom are students; or
- occupied only by one or more such persons as term time accommodation.[25]

The students in question are those who are disregarded for the purpose of a discount (see p79). This exemption does not apply to a dwelling occupied only by 'traditional' student nurses. Student nurses studying academic courses at universities or who are on Project 2000 courses do, however, count as students.[26] If the dwelling has more than one resident they both or all need to meet the qualifying conditions for the exemption to apply.

A dwelling is to be regarded as occupied by a student as term time accommodation during any vacation in which s/he:

- holds a freehold or leasehold interest in or licence to occupy the whole or any part of the dwelling; and
- has previously used or intends to use the dwelling as term time accommodation.

Example

A non-resident owner lets out her house to three students as joint tenants. It is exempt from the council tax. One of the students is dismissed from his course and therefore no longer qualifies for a status discount. The dwelling is no longer exempt. The three joint tenants are now jointly liable for the council tax on the dwelling (Chapter 6). There are three residents but two of them are disregarded for the purpose of a discount (Chapter 8). The council tax bill should be reduced by 25 per cent because there is only one adult resident who is not disregarded.

Which dwellings are exempt in Scotland?

Exhibit 5.2   Exempt dwellings: Scotland[27]

Further conditions are described in the text

An unoccupied dwelling:
- recently erected and still unfurnished;
- undergoing structural repair, improvement or reconstruction;
- owned by a charity and unoccupied for less than six months;
- unfurnished and unoccupied for less than six months;
- last occupied by someone in prison or living elsewhere to receive or provide care;
- owned by someone who has died;
- where occupation is prohibited or which is kept unoccupied pending acquisition or demolition;
- owned by a housing body prior to demolition;
- kept for occupation by a minister of religion;
- last occupied by a student;
- owned by a student;
- repossessed following a mortgage default;
- last occupied together with certain agricultural lands;
- part of the same premises as another dwelling and difficult to let separately.

Other dwellings:
- occupied only by one or more students, school or college leavers or under 18s;
- housing association 'trial' property;
- students' halls of residence;
- armed forces accommodation;
- garages, car-ports, storage sheds, etc.

Unoccupied, new dwellings

A dwelling that is unoccupied and unfurnished is exempt for up to six months if:

- the effective date for the first entry in the valuation list is later than 1 April 1993; *and*

- there was no entry in the valuation roll immediately prior to that date.[28]

These conditions are met by unoccupied, unfurnished new dwellings following their completion.

An unoccupied and unfurnished dwelling is also exempt if:

- it is entered in the valuation list with effect from 1 April 1993; *and*
- less than six months have passed since the date on which it would first have been entered in that list had that list been in force from 1 October 1992.[29]

Unoccupied dwelling undergoing structural repair, improvement or reconstruction

An unoccupied dwelling is exempt indefinitely if it is incapable of being lived in because it is being:

- structurally repaired;
- improved; *or*
- reconstructed.[30]

The reason for the lack of occupation must be the carrying out of the works. If the dwelling is actually occupied then it is not exempt.

Unoccupied dwelling owned by a charity

An unoccupied dwelling owned by a charitable body is exempt for up to six months if it was last occupied in furtherance of that body's objectives.[31] 'Charitable' has the same meaning as in the Income Tax Acts. Any period of occupation for less than six weeks is disregarded.[32]

Unoccupied and unfurnished dwelling

Unoccupied and unfurnished dwellings are exempt for up to six months from the end of the last period of six weeks or more during which the dwelling was occupied or furnished.[33]

Dwelling last occupied by someone in prison or living elsewhere to receive or provide care

An unoccupied dwelling is exempt indefinitely if it was last occupied as the sole or main residence of someone who but for this exemption would be liable; and since the last day of occupation s/he has been:

- someone who would be disregarded for the purpose of a council tax discount due to detention, or residence in a hospital, nursing or residential care home or certain care hostels in Scotland, England or Wales (Chapter 8); *or*

- receiving personal care elsewhere which is required because of her/ his old age, disablement, illness, past or present alcohol or drug dependence or past or present mental disorder; *or*
- providing personal care to someone elsewhere who needs it because of old age, disablement, illness, past or present alcohol or drug dependence, or past or present mental disorder.[34]

Any period of occupation of less than six weeks since the last day of occupation is disregarded.

Dwelling owned by someone who has died

To be exempt under this heading the dwelling must be no one's sole or main residence. Additionally any liability to pay council tax (but for this exemption) must fall to be met solely out of the estate of a deceased person.[35] In such cases the dwelling is:

- exempt indefinitely where no grant of confirmation to the estate of that person has been made; *and*
- exempt for up to six months from the date such a grant is made.

Occupation of dwelling prohibited by law

Where the occupation of a dwelling is prohibited by law it is exempt indefinitely.[36] The fact that such a property is actually occupied should not make it ineligible for the exemption.

It is also exempt indefinitely where it is kept unoccupied by reason of action taken under powers conferred by, or under, any Act of Parliament:

- with a view to prohibiting its occupation; *or*
- due to impending compulsory purchase.

In these circumstances if the dwelling is actually occupied then it should not qualify for the exemption.

Unoccupied dwelling owned by housing body prior to demolition

A housing body is defined as a district or islands council, Scottish Homes or a new town development corporation. Where an unoccupied dwelling is owned by such a body it is exempt for as long as it is kept unoccupied with a view to having it demolished.[37]

Dwelling held for a minister of religion

A dwelling, such as a manse, which is no one's sole or main residence, is exempt indefinitely if it is being held:

- by, or on behalf of, any religious body;
- for the purpose of being available for occupation by a minister of religion as a residence from which to perform the duties of the office.[38]

Dwelling repossessed by mortgage lender

A dwelling which is no one's sole or main residence is exempt indefinitely if it has been repossessed by a mortgage lender.[39]

Dwelling last occupied with agricultural lands

An unoccupied and unfurnished dwelling is exempt indefinitely if it was last used and occupied together with, and used in connection with, the lands and heritages on which the dwelling is situated and they are:

- agricultural or pastoral; *or*
- woodlands, market gardens, orchards, allotments or allotment gardens; *or*
- used for the purpose of poultry farming and exceeding one tenth of a hectare.[40]

Housing association trial property

A dwelling held by a registered housing association and used as a trial property is exempt indefinitely if:

- it is no one's sole or main residence; *and*
- it is held by a registered housing association for the purpose of being available for occupation by persons of pensionable age or disabled persons who are likely in future to have their sole or main residences in other dwellings provided by the association.[41]

Armed forces accommodation

An occupied or unoccupied dwelling is exempt indefinitely if it is:

- owned by the Secretary of State for Defence; *and*
- held for the purposes of armed forces accommodation.[42]

The authority receives compensating payments for these dwellings.

Visiting forces accommodation

A dwelling is exempt indefinitely where a member of a visiting force or a dependant of such a member (but not a dependant who is a British citizen or is ordinarily resident in the UK) would be liable.[43]

Dwelling sole or main residence of under 18s

A dwelling is exempt indefinitely if it is the sole or main residence of one or more persons under the age of 18 years and of no one else.[44]

Unoccupied dwelling difficult to let separately from another dwelling

An unoccupied dwelling, such as an empty granny flat or staff accommodation, is exempt indefinitely if:

- it forms part of premises which include another dwelling; *or*
- it is situated within the curtilage of another dwelling; *and*
- it is difficult to let separately from that other dwelling; *and*
- the person who would be liable for it (but for this exemption) has her or his sole or main residence in that other dwelling.[45]

Separate garages, car-ports, storage sheds, etc.

Certain garages, car-ports, car parking stances and premises used for storing domestic items including cycles and similar vehicles are considered to be dwellings (Chapter 2). They are exempt indefinitely from the council tax.[46]

Dwelling held by trustee in bankruptcy

A dwelling which is no one's sole or main residence is exempt indefinitely if the only person who would be liable, but for this exemption, is a trustee in bankruptcy (by virtue of subsections (1) or (10) of section 31, or subsection (6) of section 32, of the Bankruptcy (Scotland) Act 1985 as amended).[47]

Dwelling owned by student

A dwelling which is no one's sole or main residence is exempt indefinitely if the owner who would be liable (but for this exemption) counts as a student for the purpose of a council tax discount (Chapter 8). In the case of joint owners they must all be students.[48]

Dwelling occupied only by one or more students or under 18s

A dwelling is exempt indefinitely if it is not the sole or main residence of any one other than a student for the purpose of a council tax discount (Chapter 8) or a person under 18 and it is occupied by at least one such person.[49]

Student's unoccupied dwelling

An unoccupied dwelling which is a student's main residence and which was last occupied by a student or students is exempt for up to four months from the last day it was occupied for a period of six weeks or more.[50] This applies, for example, to the student's term time accommodation during vacations if the accommodation remains unoccupied during that period.

Halls of residence

A dwelling which is, or is part of, a hall of residence provided predominantly for the accommodation of students and which:

- is owned and managed by a prescribed educational institution (Exhibit 8.3) for the purpose of council tax discounts; *or*
- is the subject of an agreement allowing such an institution to nominate the majority of the persons who are to occupy the accommodation so provided.[51]

How are exempt dwellings identified?

Different authorities have used different methods to identify potentially exempt dwellings. Many used their former community charge records. Most also carried out comprehensive or targeted postal surveys. Some have used other sources of information such as education or benefit records. Authorities must continue to take reasonable steps each financial year to ascertain whether any dwellings in their areas will be, or were, exempt for any period during the year.[52] Again most are likely to carry out periodic postal surveys and make use of other sources of information such as the electoral roll and the authority's benefit records. The DoE has provided guidance on the data protection implications of the authority's use of computerised records in Practice Note No. 8. In addition to the foregoing, most authorities carry out regular visits to unoccupied exempt dwellings.

Where the authority has no reason to believe that a particular dwelling will be or was exempt it can assume that fact for council tax billing purposes.[53] Alternatively if the authority has reason to believe that a particular dwelling will be or was exempt for a period during the year, it must make that assumption for council tax billing purposes.[54]

What notification should the authority provide?

Where the authority has assumed that a dwelling is exempt it must write to the person who would otherwise be liable, informing her/him of that fact.[55] This requirement does not apply where the dwelling is held by the Secretary of State for Defence as armed forces accommodation.[56] Additionally in Scotland it does not apply where:

- the otherwise liable person is a housing body; *or*
- the dwelling is a separate garage, car-port, storage shed, etc.[57]

Where notification must be supplied this should be done as soon as reasonably practicable after the assumption has been made.[58] The authority should also supply a statement that:

- shows the valuation band for the dwelling;
- summarises how people may make proposals for altering the valuation list;
- in Scotland specifies for the financial year in question the amounts set by the authority as council tax, council water charge and in appropriate cases the district council tax;
- in England and Wales specifies the authority's estimate of the amount (or the actual amount if the year is over) which would have been payable in respect of council tax but disregarding any disability reduction, discount, transitional reduction or council tax benefit that may have been payable;
- summarises the classes of dwelling which are exempt;
- in Scotland summarises the individual's obligation to correct any incorrect assumptions the authority may have made in awarding the exemption and the £50 penalty which may be imposed if this obligation is not met.[59]

The above information need not be given if it has already been given on the introduction of the scheme or on any bill ('demand notice').[60] Additionally, where there is more than one potentially liable person the authority only has to write to one of them.[61]

How may an exemption be obtained?

Where the authority has not awarded an exemption the owner or resident may write to the authority setting out the reasons why the dwelling should be exempt. Exemptions can be backdated to the beginning of the scheme or the date the conditions for the exemption were first met, whichever is the later. Unlike the provisions for backdating most social security benefits there is no requirement for anyone to show 'good cause' for the backdating of the exemption.

The duty to correct false assumptions

The person who has been notified by the authority that the dwelling is, or will be, exempt has a duty to notify the authority if there is reason to believe that the dwelling is not exempt. The authority should be notified in writing within 21 days.[62]

This obligation to inform the authority arises at any time before the end of the financial year following the financial year in respect of which the authority's assumption about the exemption is made. In other words if the authority awards an exemption for 1993–94 and the person who would otherwise be liable for the council tax on the dwelling realises that the assumption is incorrect at any time between April 1993 and March 1995 then the authority must be informed of that fact. If however s/he only realises in April 1995 that the assumption for 1993–94 was incorrect the authority need not be informed and no penalty will be payable.

Where two or more people are jointly liable to pay council tax in respect of the dwelling and period concerned, the duty to notify the authority is a duty of each of them. Only one of them, however, has to supply the information for the obligation to be met.[63]

Penalties

The authority has the discretion to impose a penalty of £50 on the otherwise liable person who fails to notify the authority that her or his dwelling is no longer exempt.[64] An English or Welsh authority may quash such a penalty. A Scottish authority may revoke the imposition of such a penalty if the person upon whom it was imposed had a reasonable excuse for the failure.[65] Each time the authority repeats the request and the person fails to supply the information a further £200 penalty can be imposed.[66]

An appeal may be made against the imposition of a penalty (Chapter 13).[67] In England and Wales this should be done by writing directly to the valuation tribunal. In Scotland an appeal can be made to the valuation appeal committee by writing to the authority. The authority should pass the appeal on to the committee. In England and Wales an appeal to a tribunal must normally be made within two months of the penalty being imposed. The president of the tribunal has the discretion to allow an out-of-time appeal where the aggrieved person has failed to meet the time limit for reasons beyond her or his control. In Scotland the appeal must be made within two months of the penalty being imposed. There is no power to consider out-of-time appeals. If an appeal has been made then the penalty need not be paid until the appeal has been decided.

How is an appeal made against a refusal to grant an exemption?

If the authority decide that the dwelling is not exempt an appeal can be made by an aggrieved person writing to the authority.[68] There is no time limit for the making of such appeals. The aggrieved person is someone who would be liable to pay the tax if the dwelling were not exempt and also the owner if different. The appeal letter should give the reasons why the dwelling should be exempt. The authority has two months in which to answer.[69]

If an exemption is not granted, or if the authority fails to answer within two months of receipt of the appeal, a further appeal can be made (Chapter 13).[70] In England and Wales this is done by writing directly to the valuation tribunal. In Scotland it is made by writing again to the authority. The authority should pass the appeal on to the secretary of the relevant local valuation appeal committee. In England and Wales an appeal to a tribunal must normally be made within two months of the date the authority notified the aggrieved person of its decision; or within four months of the date when the initial written representation was made if the authority has not responded. The president of the tribunal has the power to allow an out-of-time appeal where the aggrieved person has failed to meet the appropriate time limit for reasons beyond her or his control. In Scotland the appeal must be made within four months of the date on which the grievance was first raised with the authority in writing. There is no power to consider an out-of-time appeal. The authority may enforce payment of the original bill while the appeal is outstanding (Chapter 12).

CHAPTER SIX

Liability

This chapter explains:

- who has to pay the tax and in Scotland the council water charge;
- how to identify the liable resident if there is more than one resident;
- the additional rules relating to residential caravans and houseboats in England and Wales;
- when the owner of a dwelling is always responsible for the tax;
- when someone is jointly liable for the tax with a resident or owner;
- how the authority identifies the liable person; *and*
- how an appeal can be made against the authority's decision on liability.

Who is liable?

The council tax is payable for any dwelling which is not exempt (Chapter 5). Additionally in Scotland the council water charge is payable for any dwelling which is not exempt except where:

- the water authority does not provide a supply of water to the dwelling; *or*
- the water is supplied by meter; *or*
- the water authority is under an obligation to provide a supply free of charge.

Exhibits 6.1 (England and Wales) and 6.3 (Scotland) identify the person who is liable. No one has to pay the tax, however, unless a bill has been sent out with his or her name on it (Chapter 11) unless they are jointly liable with someone who has been billed in Scotland. To work out who has to pay the tax on a particular dwelling examine the appropriate Exhibit. As soon as a description is reached which applies to someone in relation to the dwelling in question that person is the liable person.[1] This is normally an owner-occupier or a council, housing association or private tenant. A tenant is not liable, however, if the landlord lives in the same dwelling. If no one is solely or mainly resident in the dwelling then the non-resident owner is liable. In certain instances, however, the owner is always liable (see below).

If more than one person fits the first description that applies they will normally be jointly liable (see below). For the purpose of determining the liable person on any day the state of affairs at the end of the day is assumed to have existed throughout that day.[2]

In certain cases the liable person may also be a person who is disregarded for the purpose of a council tax discount (Chapter 8). The rules on discounts are quite separate and do not affect liability except in some cases affecting severely mentally impaired people who would otherwise be held jointly liable.

Exhibit 6.1 Hierarchy of liability: England and Wales

- A resident with a freehold interest in the whole or any part of the dwelling.
- A resident with a leasehold interest (including an assured tenancy) in the whole or any part of the dwelling which is not inferior to another such interest held by another resident
- A resident and a statutory (within the meaning of the Rent Act 1977 or the Rent (Agriculture) Act 1976) or a secure tenant (within the meaning of Part IV of the Housing Act 1985) of the whole or any part of the dwelling.[3]
- A resident with a contractual licence to occupy the whole or any part of the dwelling.
- A resident (including a squatter).
- A non-resident owner, ie the person who has the inferior (shortest) lease granted for a term of six months or more of the whole, or any part of, the dwelling. Where there is no such leaseholder the freeholder is the owner.[4]

Caravans and boats in England and Wales

Additional rules apply to residential caravans and houseboats in England and Wales. Exhibit 6.2 identifies who must pay the tax on such dwellings. The person who fits the first description that applies is the liable person.[5]

The normal council tax definition of resident and owner applies in the case of residential caravans or boats but the definition of owner is extended to include:

- the person who has possession under any hire purchase or

Exhibit 6.2   Caravans and boats: hierarchy of liability

- A resident owner.
- A resident.
- A non-resident owner.

Exhibit 6.3   Hierarchy of liability: Scotland

- A resident owner of the whole or any part of the dwelling.
- A resident tenant of the whole or any part of the dwelling.
- A resident statutory tenant (within the meaning of the Rent (Scotland) Act 1984), resident statutory assured tenant (within the meaning of the Housing (Scotland) Act 1988) or resident secure tenant (within the meaning of Part III of the Housing (Scotland) Act 1987) of the whole or any part of the dwelling.[7]
- A resident sub-tenant of the whole or any part of the dwelling.
- A resident of the dwelling *or*
- Any of the following:
  - a sub-tenant of the whole or any part of the dwelling under a sub-lease granted for a term of six months or more
  - a tenant, under a lease granted for a term of six months or more, of any part of the dwelling which is not subject to a sub-lease granted for a term of six months or more
  - an owner of any part of the dwelling which is not subject to a lease granted for a term of six months or more.

---

conditional sale agreement; *or*
- the person entitled to the property apart from any mortgage or bill of sale which applies to it.[6]

Who counts as a resident?

The council tax is usually payable by someone who is resident in the dwelling. If no one is resident then the non-resident owner is liable. To count as a 'resident' someone must:

- be aged 18 or over; *and*
- be solely or mainly resident in the dwelling.[8]

If everyone who lives in the dwelling is aged under 18 then in England and Wales the non-resident owner is liable if the dwelling does not fall into an exempt category (Chapter 5). In Scotland the dwelling is exempt from the tax (Chapter 5).

Sole or main residence

Where a potentially liable person has more than one home it will be necessary for the authority to decide which is the main residence. The concept of sole or main residence is not defined in law but was a crucial one under the community charge scheme and may be the cause of a number of council tax appeals. The Department of the Environment Community Charge Practice Note No. 9 highlighted the Oxford English Dictionary definition of reside as 'to dwell permanently or for a considerable time, to have one's settled or usual place of abode, to live in or at a particular place'. In relation to income tax and electoral law the courts have accepted that:

- residence implies a degree of permanence;
- temporary presence at an address does not make a person resident there;
- temporary absence does not deprive a person of residence;
- the lawfulness or otherwise of any home is irrelevant; *and*
- in determining whether a person not actually present at a given place is legally there it is relevant to ascertain whether that person intends to return, whether s/he is at physical liberty to return, and whether or not s/he could return without breach of any public or private obligation.

The main community charge case on this issue involved a merchant seaman, Mr Anderton, who was at sea for three months out of every four. He was found by the court to be resident on shore at his home on the grounds that a merchant ship cannot constitute someone's residence and that his house was his settled and usual abode.[9]

Example

A couple live in a house with their 17-year-old daughter. The woman is the joint owner of the property with her sister who frequently comes to stay and has a bedroom of her own, but who has her main home elsewhere. At the moment the couple living in the house would be liable for the council tax. The non-resident joint owner would not be liable.

If the couple separate and the man leaves the dwelling the woman is liable by herself but the man remains jointly liable for any amount that accrued while living as a couple.

If the woman also leaves the dwelling with the daughter as the only one living there in England and Wales the woman is still jointly liable for the tax but this time with her sister. In Scotland the dwelling would be exempt as it is the sole residence of someone under the age of 18. On the daughter's

18th birthday she becomes the sole liable person as the only resident of the dwelling.

When is the owner always liable?

Where there are no residents in the dwelling the non-resident owner is liable. Additionally, the appropriate Secretary of State has power to specify circumstances where, even if there are residents, the owner is always liable.[10] These are summarised in Exhibit 6.4. Non-owner residents in the following dwellings are not liable for the council tax.

Exhibit 6.4   Dwellings where the owner is always liable

Further conditions are described in the text

- Residential care homes and nursing homes.
- Certain hostels providing care and support.
- Houses of religious communities.
- Houses in multiple occupation.
- Second homes with domestic servants.
- Residences of ministers of religion.
- School boarding accommodation (Scotland).

Nursing, residential care homes and certain hostels

The particular dwellings in question are as defined for the purposes of a discount (Chapter 8).

Religious communities

To fit this definition the dwelling must be inhabited by a religious community whose principal occupation consists of prayer, contemplation, education, the relief of suffering, or any combination of these.[11] Monasteries and convents fit within this description. Members of such communities may qualify to be disregarded for the purpose of a council tax discount (Chapter 8).

Houses in multiple occupation

To fall within this class the dwelling must have been originally constructed, or subsequently adapted for occupation by more than one household.[12] In addition each person who lives in it must be either:

- a tenant or licensee able to occupy only part of the dwelling; *or*
- a licensee liable to pay rent or a licence fee on only part of the dwelling.

Examples of this type of accommodation include some bed-sits, hostels, nurses' homes and long-stay wards in hospitals where they are classed as dwellings. It should be noted that despite its title this class can include a dwelling occupied by only one person if the above conditions are met so long as the dwelling was originally constructed, or subsequently adapted, for occupation by multiple households.

The term 'tenant' includes a secure tenant or a statutory tenant and includes those leaseholders whose interest is granted for six months or more. 'Secure' and 'statutory tenant' are defined in Exhibits 6.1 and 6.3.

In England and Wales the normal definition of an owner applies in the case of a house in multiple occupation except that where someone has a leasehold interest it must be an interest in the whole of the dwelling. If this is not the case the liability falls upon the person who has a freehold interest in the whole or any part of the dwelling.[13]

The landlord may, if the correct procedures are followed, pass on the cost of the council tax in the form of a rent increase. While residents faced with such an increase are not able to obtain assistance via any of the methods discussed in Chapters 7, 8 or 9, they may be eligible for help via the housing benefit scheme as the increase in rent is treated as an eligible cost for that benefit.

Second homes with domestic servants

A dwelling fits into this category if it is:

- occupied from time to time by the employer who does not live in it as a main residence; *and*
- all the residents are either employed in domestic service in the dwelling or a family member of such an employee.[14]

Ministers of religion

To fit this category the dwelling must be inhabited by a minister of religion (of any faith) as a residence from which to perform the duties of the office.[15] If the dwelling is owned by the minister then it is the minister who is liable. The one exception to this rule is where an English or Welsh dwelling is owned by a minister of the Church of England. In such a case the liability is transferred to the Diocesan Board of Finance rather than to the owner.

School boarding accommodation

In Scotland the owner of school boarding accommodation which is specifically included within the definition of a dwelling (Chapter 2) is liable for the council tax.[16]

Who is jointly liable?

Where two or more people fall into the liable category, for example joint owners, joint tenants or simply joint residents, they are jointly and severally liable with the exception of someone who is severely mentally impaired (see below).[17] Additionally the liable person's partner of the opposite sex is jointly liable if s/he is:

- married to the liable person; *or*
- living with her/his partner as husband and wife; *and*
- a resident of the dwelling.[18]

This applies whether or not the partner has a legal interest in the dwelling. The definition of 'couple' used in establishing joint liability for the council tax is almost the same as that which applies for many social security benefits (eg council tax benefit). Under the social security rules, however, to be a couple both partners must reside in the same *household* – whereas under the council tax it is only necessary to show that they reside in the same *dwelling*. As it is possible for a single dwelling to contain more than one separate household, there will be some situations where the two definitions do not exactly coincide. An obvious case arises where a married couple are estranged and continue to reside in the same dwelling but within completely separate households. For council tax purposes they will still be classed as a jointly liable couple since they remain married and both continue to reside in the same *dwelling*. But they will not be a couple for council tax benefit purposes since, despite being married, they reside in different *households*. This means that both partners will be jointly liable but that each will be able to make a separate claim for council tax benefit based on an apportioned (50 per cent) share of council tax liability (see p108) and their own individual circumstances.

The expression 'living together as husband and wife' uses exactly the same form of words for both council tax and social security purposes, but is not defined within the legislation in either case. However, there is a substantial body of social security case-law on the various criteria which must be considered when attempting to establish whether two people are living together as husband and wife (see p115) and, arguably, this will be highly persuasive in council tax cases also. The above discrepancy between the council tax and social security definitions of a 'couple' is unlikely to occur in the case of *unmarried* couples, therefore, since in this case the council tax rules require both that the parties must be living together as husband and wife *and* that they reside in the same dwelling. It is difficult to see how the authority could conclude that two unmarried persons are living together as husband and wife unless they were, in fact, members of the same household (as opposed to merely being resident in the same dwelling). This is because, according to established case-law, a key finding of fact which must be made before an authority is entitled to conclude that two unmarried persons are living together as husband and wife is that they are members of the same household.

Joint liability does not apply to homosexual couples unless they are also joint owners, tenants, etc. Practice Note No. 2 (para 18) points out that in polygamous marriages all partners resident in the dwelling are jointly liable.

Again this joint liability does not apply where the partner is disregarded for the purposes of a council tax discount because of a severe mental impairment (see below).

The significance of joint liability

The authority has the option of addressing the council tax bill to one of the jointly liable people or all of them. In Scotland someone who is jointly liable with the person or persons named on the bill but whose name is not included is still liable to make the required payments (Chapter 11), In England and Wales no payment can be required from a liable person until s/he has been billed. Practice Note No. 2 (para 20) advises English and Welsh authorities to include on bills the names of as many liable persons as possible. This allows the authority to take recovery action against any or all of them. If the authority want to recover the council tax from someone who is jointly liable but not named on the original bill a fresh bill (a joint taxpayers' notice) must be issued.[19]

To be eligible for council tax benefit the claimant has also to be liable for the council tax. Where someone other than the claimant's partner is jointly liable for the tax council tax benefit is worked out on the claimant's apportioned share even though the authority may be seeking to recover all of the council tax due from one person (Chapter 10). Where the claimant is in receipt of council tax benefit the late identification of retrospective joint liability gives rise to an overpayment of benefit and the potential for a late claim for benefit from the newly identified jointly liable person (Chapter 10).

Joint liability and severe mental impairment

The one exception to the rule on joint liability relates to someone who is disregarded for the purpose of working out a discount because of a severe mental impairment (Chapter 8). Such a person is not held jointly liable if there is someone else with the same status and legal interest in the property who is not severely mentally impaired.[20] A severely mentally impaired person is liable for the tax however if:

- s/he is the only liable person; *or*
- s/he is the only owner tenant or contractual licensee even if the partner is not severely mentally impaired; *or*
- all the jointly liable people are severely mentally impaired.

Additionally a liable person's partner is not liable if severely mentally impaired.

Example

A couple are joint owners of a house. The man counts as severely mentally impaired and is disregarded for the purpose of a council tax discount. Normally the couple as joint owners and residents would be liable but as the man is severely mentally impaired the woman is liable. If she were no longer to reside in the dwelling the severely mentally impaired man would become liable. He would still be disregarded for the purpose of working out a council tax discount.

What happens if circumstances change?

A change of circumstances may alter or change the tax liability during the year. For example a liable owner may sell the dwelling or a liable tenant may move to live elsewhere. Liability for the council tax arises on a daily basis and the state of affairs at the end of the day is assumed to have lasted all that day.[21] Consequently the liable person is liable for the first day of residence in the dwelling but not the last. Where a liable person dies there is no liability for any part of the day on which she or he dies.

How does the authority identify the liable person?

In order to establish liability the authority has a variety of powers to require people and organisations to provide information. It is also able to use its own information obtained for other purposes. If the authority is unable to identify a liable person by name it may serve a bill on 'The Council Tax Payer'. The residents of the dwelling then need to decide who has to pay the tax.

Use of the authority's own information

An authority may use information obtained under any other enactment provided in England and Wales that it was not obtained in its role as a police authority and in Scotland that it is not information obtained through social work activities unless it consists solely of names and addresses.[22] It is this rule which enabled authorities to use their community charge and other records to establish a database of liable persons. Practice Note No. 5 (para 1.1) reminds authorities, however, to bear in mind the provisions of the Data Protection Act 1984 when considering using the information they hold on computer. Practice Note No. 8 examines data protection issues and council tax administration.

Information that must be provided by residents, owners or managing agents

The authority has the power to write to anyone who appears to be a resident, owner or managing agent of a particular dwelling requesting information it requires for the purpose of identifying the liable person or the person who would be liable if the dwelling were not exempt.[23] A 'managing agent' means any person authorised to arrange lettings of the dwelling concerned. In practice most authorities carried out a postal survey prior to the commencement of the scheme to help identify liable persons. In the future such enquiries are likely to be on an individual basis. The person who receives such a written enquiry must supply the required information within 21 days of receipt if it is in her or his possession or control.

Penalties

The authority has the discretion to impose a penalty of £50 on someone who fails to respond to a request for information for the purpose of identifying the liable person.[24] An English or Welsh authority may quash such a penalty. A Scottish authority may revoke the imposition of such a penalty if the person upon whom it was imposed had a reasonable excuse for the failure to supply it.[25] Each time the authority repeats the request and the person fails to supply the information another £200 penalty can be imposed.[26]

Appeals against the imposition of a penalty

An appeal may be made against the imposition of a penalty (Chapter

13).[27] In England and Wales this should be done by writing directly to the valuation tribunal. In Scotland an appeal can be made to the valuation appeal committee by writing to the authority who should pass the appeal on to the committee. In England and Wales an appeal to a tribunal must normally be made within two months of the penalty being imposed. The president of the tribunal has the discretion to allow an out-of-time appeal where the aggrieved person has failed to meet the time limit for reasons beyond her/his control. In Scotland the appeal must be made within two months of the penalty being imposed. There is no power to consider out-of-time appeals.[28] If an appeal has been made then the penalty need not be paid until the appeal has been decided.

Information that must be supplied by other public bodies

The authority has the power to make a written request for information to:

- any billing authority;
- any precepting authority;
- any levying authority;
- the electoral registration officer for any area in Great Britain; *and*
- any community charges registration officer.[29]

In Scotland information may also be requested from the local assessor, a district council, Scottish Homes or a new town development corporation.[30]

The authority cannot however request information from an organisation if that organisation obtained it in its capacity as:

- a police authority;
- a constituent council of a police authority; *or*
- an employer.

Additionally the authority cannot request information which consists of anything more than:

- a name;
- an address;
- any past or present place of residence of any person; *and*
- the dates during which that person is known or thought to have resided there.

In the case of the community charge registration officer the authority can also request information about the status of individuals exempt from the personal community charge. This is particularly useful in identifying those who are severely mentally impaired.

The information must be supplied within 21 days of receipt of the request if it is in the organisation's possession or control.

An authority may supply relevant information to another authority even if it has not been requested.

Information as to deaths

Within seven days of the registration of the death of any person aged 18 or over, the registrar of births and deaths for the area in which the death occurred must supply the relevant information to the appropriate authority.[31]

How is an appeal made against a decision on liability?

If the authority decides that someone is liable or jointly liable for the council tax an appeal may be made against the decision by an aggrieved person writing to the authority.[32] There is no time limit for the making of such appeals. The aggrieved person is someone who is considered liable to pay the tax and also the owner if different. The appeal letter should give the reasons why the authority has come to the wrong decision. The authority has two months in which to answer.[33]

If the authority refuses to alter its decision or fails to answer within two months of receipt of the appeal, a further appeal can be made (Chapter 13).[34] In England and Wales this is done by writing directly to the valuation tribunal. In Scotland such a further appeal is made by writing again to the authority. The authority should pass the appeal on to the secretary of the relevant local valuation appeal committee. In England and Wales an appeal to a tribunal must normally be made within two months of the date the authority notified the aggrieved person of its decision; or within four months of the date when the initial written representation was made if the authority has not responded. The president of the tribunal has the power to allow an out-of-time appeal where the aggrieved person has failed to meet the appropriate time limits for reasons beyond her/his control. In Scotland the appeal must be made within four months of the date on which the grievance was first raised with the authority in writing. There is no power to consider an out-of-time appeal.[35] The authority may enforce payment of the original bill while the appeal is outstanding (Chapter 12).

CHAPTER SEVEN

Disability reductions

This chapter explains:

- the conditions that must be met for a disability reduction to be awarded;
- who is entitled to the reduction;
- how an application is made;
- the information that must be provided;
- how the reduction should be made;
- the effect of the reduction on other forms of help with the tax; *and*
- how an appeal may be made against the authority's decision not to grant a disability reduction.

Disability reduction schemes apply in England and Wales[1] and in Scotland.[2] The basic amount of the council tax, and in Scotland the council water charge,[3] may be reduced where:

- a disabled person lives in the dwelling; *and*
- the dwelling has certain attributes that are essential or of major importance to the disabled person because of her/his disability.

The reduction may be applied for in respect of residential care or nursing homes as well as any other dwelling. Dwellings in the lowest band (band A), however, do not qualify for a disability reduction.

In addition to the disability reduction scheme the value of fixtures designed to make the dwelling suitable for use by a physically disabled person should have been ignored in the valuation of the dwelling if they added to its value (Chapter 3). Where fixtures designed to make the dwelling suitable for use by a physically disabled person reduce the value of the dwelling they should have been taken into account in the valuation process and therefore reflected in the dwelling's banding.[4]

What are the conditions for a disability reduction?

The disabled person

For the reduction to be awarded the dwelling must be the sole or main residence of at least one disabled person. The concept of sole or main residence is examined in Chapter 6. No additional reduction is made if more than one disabled person resides in the dwelling.

To count as disabled for the purpose of the reduction someone must be substantially and permanently disabled (whether by illness, injury, congenital deformity or otherwise). The disabled person may be an adult or a child. S/he need not be a person liable to pay the council tax on the dwelling.

Social security authorities have a separate duty (via social services departments in England and Wales and social work departments in Scotland) to maintain a register of, and provide various services to, persons resident in their area who are substantially and permanently disabled. The social work authorities involved have considerably more skills and experience in making assessments of disability than their counterparts in council tax administration. Inclusion on the disabled person's register would therefore be highly indicative that a person satisfies the criteria of 'substantially and permanently disabled' for the purposes of a disability reduction (although non-inclusion should not automatically lead to the opposite conclusion – since such registers are not comprehensive and inclusion on them is not compulsory).

The dwelling

The dwelling must have at least one of the following attributes:

- a room, but not a bathroom, a kitchen or a lavatory, which is predominantly used (whether for providing therapy or otherwise) by the disabled person; or
- an additional bathroom or kitchen within the dwelling; or
- sufficient floor space to permit the use of a wheelchair.

To qualify, however, the attribute must be essential, or of major importance to the disabled person's well-being because of the nature of her/his disability. It should be noted that a sole bathroom or kitchen, even if specially adapted to meet the needs of a disabled person, is not sufficient to qualify. Additionally a wheelchair is not considered to be required for meeting the disabled person's needs if s/he does not need to use it within the living accommodation comprising or included in the dwelling concerned. A reduction may be awarded, for example, where the dwelling has an extension used for dialysis equipment. It should be emphasised, however, that a dwelling does not need to have been extended or adapted to have any of the above attributes. For example, if a downstairs room in a two-storey house must be used as a bedroom because of the disabled person's disability it would qualify as a room predominantly used by the disabled person even though it has not been specially built or adapted for her or him.

Who can obtain the reduction?

The person entitled to the reduction is the person liable to pay the council tax on the dwelling. The individual may be solely liable or jointly liable. Where there is joint liability an application made by one of the liable persons is treated as also made on behalf of each of them. None of the liable persons need be disabled.

The authority may also award a disability reduction to someone who will be liable for the council tax on the dwelling – perhaps, for example, following work to the dwelling associated with the needs of a disabled person.

How is an application made?

The authority cannot award a reduction without a written application for each financial year (April–March) from the liable person or someone acting on her or his behalf. Most authorities have standard application forms for this purpose. Practice Note No. 2 (Annex C) contains a model form that authorities may use.

Backdating and repeat applications

The fact that a written application must be made for each financial year does not preclude the making of an application for previous years, ie back to the beginning of the council tax scheme or to the date when the qualifying conditions were met. The year or years in question, must however be identified on the application.

Once a written application has been made a repeat application is required each financial year. It is hoped that authorities will send people receiving the reduction a repeat application form, and a reminder, at the appropriate time each year. There is, however, nothing in the regulations that requires this though again the reduction may be backdated once the application is received. Practice

Note No. 2 (para 41) suggests that authorities should generally not require a full application in a second or subsequent year. It will often be sufficient to seek the liable person's confirmation that the circumstances have not changed since the original application.

Information required by the authority

In considering whether or not the reduction applies the English or Welsh authority may make a written request at any time to anyone for information it reasonably requires. It may also require that person to respond within a specified period but must give them at least 21 days to answer. Most authorities require a medical certificate or a supporting letter from a doctor, occupational therapist or social worker confirming that the disabled person needs the particular qualifying attribute of the dwelling because of her/his disability. The majority of authorities also visit the dwelling but only a minority make use of social service records.

How is the reduction made?

If a disability reduction is awarded the liable person's council tax bill is reduced to that of a dwelling in the valuation band immediately below the band to which the dwelling has been allocated on the valuation list. The reduction applies for each day that the qualifying conditions are met.

Example

The liable person's dwelling is shown as in band C on the valuation list. Following the award of a disability reduction the bill that must be paid should be the same as that of someone liable for the tax on a band B dwelling.

The disability reduction does not alter the actual valuation of the dwelling nor its banding on the valuation list. The liable person's bill should show both the dwelling's actual band and the reduction.

Had the dwelling been in band A then no reduction could apply since this is already the lowest band possible.

What is the effect of the reduction on other forms of help?

Someone entitled to a disability reduction may also be entitled to a discount, a transitional reduction and council tax benefit. These other forms of help are calculated on the basis of the council tax liability after the disability reduction has been made. Consequently the retrospective award of a disability reduction may result in a recoverable council tax benefit overpayment.

Change in circumstances

Future changes, for example the disabled person's move to alternative accommodation, may mean that the liable person is no longer entitled to a disability reduction. Where the liable person has reason to believe that she or he has ceased to be eligible for the reduction the authority must be notified of that belief. This obligation extends to all who are jointly liable for the tax on the dwelling in question.

How is an appeal made against a decision not to award a disability reduction?

If the authority decides not to award a disability reduction an appeal may be made against that decision by the aggrieved person writing to the authority.[5] There is no time limit for the making of such appeals. The aggrieved person is someone who is liable to pay the tax and also the owner if different. The appeal letter should give the reasons why the authority has come to the wrong decision. The authority has two months in which to answer.[6]

If the authority refuses to alter its decision or fails to answer within two months of receipt of the appeal, a further appeal can be made (Chapter 13).[7] In England and Wales this is done by writing directly to the valuation tribunal. In Scotland such a further appeal is made by writing again to the authority. The authority should pass the appeal on to the secretary of the relevant local valuation appeal committee. In England and Wales this must normally be done within two months of the date the authority notified the aggrieved person of its decision or within four months of the date when the initial representation was made if the authority has not responded. The president of the tribunal has the power to allow an out-of-time appeal where the aggrieved person has failed to meet the appropriate time limits for reasons beyond his or her control. In Scotland the appeal must be made within four months of the date on which the grievance was first raised with the authority in writing. There is no power to consider an out-of-time appeal.[8] The authority may enforce payment of the original bill while the appeal is outstanding (Chapter 12).

CHAPTER EIGHT

Discounts

This chapter explains:

- when a discount is granted;
- who is disregarded for the purpose of a discount;
- how authorities know when a discount should be granted;
- how an application for a discount may be made; *and*
- how an appeal may be made against the authority's refusal to grant a discount.

When should a discount be granted?

The council tax, and in Scotland also the council water charge, payable on a dwelling is initially based on the assumption that there are at least two adults residing in the dwelling. The bill does not increase if there are more than two but should be reduced by:

- 25 per cent if there is only one person solely or mainly resident in the dwelling; *or*
- 50 per cent in England and Scotland if no one is solely or mainly resident (this is also normally the case in Wales but special rules apply in some cases – see below).[1]

Certain people, however, are ignored or discounted when deciding how many people are solely or mainly resident in the dwelling. For the purpose of deciding for any day whether the council tax is subject to a discount the state of affairs at the end of the day is assumed to have existed throughout that day.[2] Discounts can apply to empty dwellings or second homes. Certain empty dwellings, however, are exempt from the tax (Chapter 5). A discount may follow the end of an exemption.

Example

An unoccupied and unfurnished dwelling qualifies for a six-month exemption. If the dwelling is still unoccupied at the end of the six-month period it no longer qualifies for the exemption but the full tax bill should be reduced by a 50 per cent discount.

Wales

In Wales most classes of unoccupied dwelling also qualify for a 50 per cent discount but each Welsh authority may decide that a 25 per cent discount, or no discount at all, applies where a furnished dwelling is no one's sole or main residence for six months.[3] This description typically applies to a second home. If the authority makes such a determination it must apply to all such dwellings in its area. It cannot, however, apply to a pitch occupied by a caravan or a mooring occupied by a houseboat. Additionally it does not apply:

- where someone is liable for the tax on such a dwelling only in her/ his capacity as a personal representative (ie the executor of a will) and either no grant of probate or of letters of administration has been made, or less than 12 months have elapsed since the day on which such a grant was made; or
- where the liable person is also a liable person of another dwelling which is job related as defined in the relevant regulations.[4]

Where a Welsh authority has made a decision to alter the discounts available on second homes it must publicise it in at least one newspaper circulating in its area within 21 days of making the decision. Failure to comply with this requirement, however, does not make the decision invalid.[5] Where such a decision has been made for any financial year it may be varied or revoked at any time before the beginning of that year.

A Welsh authority's decision about the application of a discount to a class of dwelling cannot be the subject of an appeal to a valuation tribunal. It may however be challenged via an application for judicial review.[6] A person may, however, appeal in the normal way (see below) against the authority's decision that a dwelling is within a class of dwelling that has been prescribed.

Discounts and other forms of help

The liable person may be granted a discount in addition to any disability reduction, transitional reduction or council tax benefit. The discount is applied to the tax after the grant of any disability reduction but prior to the calculation of a transitional reduction or main council tax benefit. Second adult rebate is worked out on the basis of the council tax liability ignoring any discount that has been granted (Chapter 10).

Who is ignored for the purposes of a discount?

Only adults solely or mainly resident in the dwelling count for the purpose of working out whether or not a discount applies. Consequently people under 18 and those solely or mainly resident elsewhere should be ignored.[7]

Examples

The only people who live in the dwelling are a lone parent and her 15-year-old daughter. There is only one person aged 18 or over residing in the dwelling. A 25 per cent discount is granted.

The lone parent's friend comes to live with her but retains a home elsewhere. If the friend can be said to be mainly resident in the lone parent's dwelling the discount no longer applies from the day the previous circumstances changed.

Who is disregarded for the purposes of a discount?

In addition to those who are ignored certain categories of people are disregarded.[8] They are listed in Exhibit 8.1. They are sometimes described as 'having a status discount' or more simply as 'invisible'.

Exhibit 8.1   People disregarded for the purposes of discount

In all cases there are further conditions described in the text

- People under 19 if child benefit is payable.
- Recent school and college leavers under 20.
- Students under the age of 20 studying up to A level, the higher grade of the Scottish Certificate of Education or equivalent.
- Full time students attending a college or university.
- Foreign language assistants.
- Student nurses.
- Apprentices.
- Youth training trainees.
- Persons in prison and other forms of detention.
- The severely mentally impaired.
- Certain carers.
- Hospital patients.

continued

Exhibit 8.1   *continued*

- People in residential care homes, nursing homes and hostels providing a high level of care.
- Members of international headquarters and defence organisations.
- Members of visiting forces.
- Members of religious communities.
- Residents in certain hostels and night shelters and other accommodation for those with no fixed abode (England and Wales only).

Status discounts and tax bills

If someone is disregarded for the purpose of a discount it does not necessarily mean that the tax bill is reduced. It is only if the number of adults residing in the dwelling is less than two, not counting any of those who are disregarded, that a discount is awarded. A liable person may be disregarded for the purpose of a discount but is still liable for the council tax. The one exception to this last rule concerns liable people who are considered to be severely mentally impaired and thus disregarded for the purpose of a discount (Chapter 6).

Examples

Two adult women are joint owner-occupiers. One is a full-time student and disregarded for the purpose of a discount. The other is in full-time work and is not disregarded. As there are only two residents and one of them is disregarded a 25 per cent discount should be granted. As joint resident owners both the student and the person in full-time employment are jointly liable for the reduced amount of council tax.

A couple in their 50s are joint owner-occupiers of a house. Their daughter lives with them. She is aged 20 and a full-time student. Their son aged 17 also lives with them. He is in full-time work. The daughter, as a full-time student, is disregarded for the purpose of a discount and the son as someone under 18 is ignored. Nevertheless no discount is awarded because two adults – the joint owner-occupiers – live in the house and are not ignored or discounted.

A pensioner couple are liable joint tenants. No one else lives with them. One of the couple has Alzheimer's disease and gets the care component of the disability living allowance. He is considered to be severely mentally impaired. In these circumstances a 25 per cent discount is awarded because there are only two people solely or mainly resident in the dwelling and one of them is disregarded for the purpose of a discount. In this instance only the joint tenant who is not severely mentally impaired is liable for the tax.

An adult carer introduced by a charity comes to live with the couple. The couple provide free accommodation plus £50 a week to the carer. In these circumstances the couple lose their discount as there are now two adults living in the dwelling who are not disregarded for the purpose of a discount. If the carer had received £30 a week or less however the discount would have continued as there would still have been only one adult living in the dwelling who was not disregarded for discount purposes.

What are the conditions for specific status discounts?

The following paragraphs set out the main conditions for each group.

Persons aged 18 and child benefit payable

A person falls into this category if aged 18 and someone else is entitled to child benefit for her/him or would be if s/he were not in local authority care.[9]

The conditions of entitlement to child benefit are described in CPAG's *Rights Guide to Non-Means-Tested Benefits 1993–94*, pp150–5. A child ceases to qualify for child benefit the week after becoming 19 or on the Sunday after the first of the following dates after leaving school or college:

- first Monday in January;
- first Monday after Easter Monday;
- first Monday in September.

School and college leavers

A person who is under the age of 20; and has left school or college on or after 1 May in any year after undertaking a qualifying course of education (ie one no higher than GCE A level, the higher grade of the Scottish Certificate of Education or equivalent) or additionally in England and Wales full-time education should be disregarded for the purpose of working out a discount during the period 1 May and 31 October in the same year.[10] Such people may continue to be disregarded if they go on to some other form of further or higher education (see below).

Who counts as a student or a student nurse?

A person is disregarded for the purposes of discount if s/he is a student.[11] A person counts as a 'student' if:

- under 20, studying for more than three months and at least 12 hours a week for any qualification up to A level or higher Scottish Certificate of Education or equivalent;
- undertaking a college or university course lasting at least one academic year, or in Scotland a specified course which takes at least 24 weeks a year and involves at least 21 hours of study a week during term time; *or*
- a foreign language assistant.[12]

A 'student nurse' undertaking 'traditional' hospital-based training does not count as a student but falls into a separate disregarded category described below. Student nurses studying academic courses at universities or who are on Project 2000 courses do count as students.[13]

An empty dwelling owned by a student, a dwelling with only student residents and hall of residence in which students reside are exempt dwellings for council tax purposes (Chapter 5).

Students under 20 undertaking a qualifying course of education (A level or equivalent)

To be disregarded under this heading the person must be undertaking a qualifying course of education.[14] A qualifying course of education is one:

- which lasts for more than three calendar months;
- which is at or below the following standards or equivalent: A level, ONC or OND, the higher grade of the Scottish Certificate of Education, National Certificate of the Scottish Vocational Educational Council or Scottish Vocational Qualification Level III;
- which is not a correspondence course;
- which is not undertaken as a result of the person's office or employment; *and*
- which in terms of tuition, supervised exercises, experiments, project or practical work etc., is normally carried out between 8.00 am and 5.30 pm (to the extent that such activities have to be carried out at a particular time).[15]

The person is considered to be undertaking such a course on a particular day if:

- s/he is under the age of 20;
- the relevant number of hours per week for that course, or where two or more such courses are being taken at the same establishment, the combined number of hours per week, exceeds 12 (excluding any vacation period).[16]

A person is undertaking such a course throughout both term time and vacations from the date the course begins to the date it is completed, abandoned or the individual is dismissed from it. The person is no longer considered to be undertaking such a course if s/he becomes an apprentice or a youth training trainee.[17]

Who counts as a full-time student?

In England and Wales to be disregarded under this heading the person must be undertaking a full-time course of education. In Scotland the key rules are similar but the student must be undertaking a specified course of education.[18]

England and Wales

To be treated as undertaking a full-time course of education the person must be enrolled for the purpose of attending such a course with a prescribed educational establishment (Exhibit 8.2). These educational establishments are the same as apply for the purpose of student hall of residence exemptions (Chapter 5).

Exhibit 8.2   Prescribed educational establishments: England and Wales

- A university including a constituent college, school or other institution of a university.
- A central institution or college of education in Scotland within the meaning of section 135(1) of the Education (Scotland) Act 1980.
- A college of education in Northern Ireland within the meaning of Article 2(2) of SI 1986 No. 594 the Education and Libraries (Northern Ireland) Order 1986.
- An institution within the PCFC (Polytechnics and Colleges Funding Council) funding sector for the purposes of section 120(8) of the Education Reform Act 1988.
- A theological college.
- Any other institution in England or Wales established solely or mainly for the purpose of providing courses of further or higher education.
- Any other institution in Scotland or Northern Ireland established solely or mainly for the purpose of providing courses of further education.[19]

A Ministry of Defence training establishment for the armed forces does not count as an educational establishment for this purpose.[20] Further education in England or Wales has the same meaning as in the Education Act 1944 (as amended). In Scotland it has the same meaning as in the Education (Scotland) Act 1980 (as amended). In Northern Ireland it has the same meaning as in article 5(c) of SI 1986 No. 594, the Education and Libraries (Northern Ireland) Order 1986. Higher education has the meaning given by section 120(1) of the Education Reform Act 1988.[21]

Full-time course of education

A full-time course of education is one:

- which lasts for at least one academic year of the educational establishment concerned, or where the establishment does not have academic years, for at least one calendar year;
- which normally requires attendance (either at the establishment or elsewhere) for periods of at least 24 weeks in each academic or calendar year (as the case may be) during which it lasts; *and*
- normally requiring at least 21 hours a week during the periods of attendance of periods of study, tuition or work experience or a combination of such periods.

A course does not count as a full-time course of education if the combined periods of work experience normally required to be undertaken as part of it exceed the combined periods of study or tuition. People are treated as undertaking work experience if, as part of the curriculum of the course they:

- are at their work place providing services under a contract of employment; *or*
- are at a place where a trade, business, profession or other occupation which is relevant to the subject matter of the course is carried on for the purposes of gaining experience of that trade, etc.[22]

For the purpose of working out the number of weeks of attendance in the year the following rules are adopted. Where the course starts at the beginning of an academic year:

- the first calendar year of the course is treated as beginning with the day on which the course begins; *and*
- subsequent calendar years (if any) are treated as beginning on the anniversary of that day.

Where the course begins part-way through an academic year:

- the academic year is treated as beginning at the beginning of the term in which the course begins; *and*
- subsequent academic years (if any) are treated as beginning at the beginning of the equivalent terms in those years.

The last part of a course which lasts (or is treated as lasting) for other than a number of complete academic or calendar years is disregarded.[23]

Scotland

In Scotland the key rules are the same, ie the student must be required to attend the course for at least 24 weeks in each academic year at a prescribed educational establishment (Exhibit 8.3) and the course must require at least 21 hours of study, tuition or work experience in each of those weeks. In addition, however, the course must be a specified course (Exhibit 8.4).[24]

Foreign language assistant

A foreign language assistant counts as a student if s/he is:

- registered with the Central Bureau for Educational Visits and Exchanges; *and*
- appointed as a foreign language assistant at a school or other educational institution in Great Britain.[27]

Student nurse

A person counts as a student nurse if studying for her/his first inclusion on the Nursing Register.[28] Nurses already on the Register but taking further courses, eg midwifery or health visiting, are not disregarded. Student nurses studying academic courses at universities or on Project 2000 are considered to be full-time students and are disregarded under that heading.

For nurses a prescribed educational establishment is:

- a college of nursing and midwifery; *or*
- a college of health.

established by a regional or a district health authority in England and Wales or a Health Board in Scotland.[29]

The relevant period for a course or programme means the period beginning with the day on which a person begins that course or programme and ending with the day on which s/he completes it, abandons it or is dismissed from it (which period includes any periods of vacation between terms and before the last day).

Exhibit 8.3   Prescribed educational establishments: Scotland[25]

- A university in the United Kingdom and any college, school, hall or other institution of such a university.
- A central institution.
- A designated institution.
- A college of nursing and midwifery or a college of health, established by a Health Board or by a Regional or District Health authority.
- Any other institution in Scotland for the provision of any form of further education (other than a Ministry of Defence training establishment for the armed forces).
- An establishment of further education in England or Wales maintained or assisted by a local education authority within the meaning of the Education Act 1944 or in receipt of grants made under regulations made under section 10 of that Act.
- Any other institution in England or Wales which is:
  - within the further education sector (in terms of subsection (3) of section 91 of the Further and Higher Education Act 1992 *or*
  - within the higher education sector (in terms of subsection (5) of that section).
- A college of education within the meaning of Article 2(2) of the Education and Libraries (Northern Ireland) Order 1986.
- An institution of further education in Northern Ireland provided by an Education and Library Board constituted in accordance with Schedule 1 to that Order.
- A theological college.
- An institution of a Research Council established by Royal Charter under section 1 of the Science and Technology Act 1965.

Evidence of student status

In considering whether someone may be disregarded as a student the authority may ask for a student certificate. With the exception of foreign language assistants, prescribed educational institutions (see above) are required to provide such certificates when requested to do so by a student or student nurse.[30]

Certificates need not be supplied, however, where the person making it stopped following a course at that institution more than a year previously. Practice Note No. 2 (p27), reminds authorities that certificates are not required as they were under the community charge

---

Exhibit 8.4 Specified courses: Scotland[26]

Courses at first degree and diploma level
- A course at undergraduate level leading to:
  - a degree, certificate, diploma or licentiateship of a university or theological college *or*
  - a degree, certificate or diploma granted by a designated institution, a central institution or any other institution for the provision of any form of further education.

Courses in further education
- A course in further education leading to an award of the Scottish Certificate of Education, the General Certificate of Education, the General Certificate of Secondary Education or the International Baccalaureate.
- A course in further education leading to the National Certificate, the Higher National Certificate or Higher National Diploma of the Scottish Vocational Education Council, or a Scottish Vocational Qualification, or any other course in further education leading to a comparable award.
- A course in further education required by an educational establishment to be undertaken prior to any other course mentioned in this Exhibit being undertaken.

Training for teaching, social work or youth and community work
- A course at undergraduate or postgraduate level for the initial training of teachers, social workers or youth and community work.

Vocational courses at postgraduate level
- A course at postgraduate level leading to a certificate or diploma in professional studies or to any other comparable award.

Courses at higher degree level
- A course leading to the award of the degree of Doctor of Philosophy or a Master's degree or to any other comparable award.

---

and that it is for authorities to decide what evidence they need.
The certificate should include the following information:

- the educational establishment's name and address;
- the full name of the person to whom it is issued;
- the student's date of birth where this is known to the establishment

and where the person is or was a student under 20 studying a course no higher than A level or equivalent;

- a statement certifying that s/he is following or has followed a course of education as a student or student nurse;
- the date when the person became a student or a student nurse at the establishment and the date when her/his course has come or is expected to come to an end.[31]

Apprentice

An apprentice is someone:

- employed for the purpose of learning a trade, business, profession, office, employment or vocation;
- for that purpose undertaking a programme of training leading to a qualification accredited by the National Council for Vocational Qualifications or the Scottish Vocational Education Council; *and*
- employed at a salary or in receipt of an allowance or both, which are, in total, substantially less than the salary likely to be received if the qualification in question had been obtained; and no more than £130 per week before any deductions for income tax, national insurance, etc.[32]

Youth training trainee

A youth training trainee is disregarded for the purpose of a discount if:

- under the age of 25; *and*
- receiving training in line with an individual training plan under the Youth Training Scheme.[33]

The trainee is regarded as undertaking training from the day on which that course or programme begins to the day it is completed or she or he abandons it or is dismissed from it.

Persons in prison and other forms of detention

In many cases persons in prison or some other form of detention are considered no longer solely or mainly resident in a dwelling and should therefore be ignored for the purpose of a discount. Dwellings left empty by those in detention are exempt from the council tax (Chapter 5). In certain instances, however, the period of detention may be for such a short period that the person in detention is still considered mainly to occupy the dwelling. In such circumstances a disregard for the purpose of a discount applies if s/he is:

- detained in a prison, a hospital or any other place by virtue of an order of a court in the United Kingdom or a Standing Civilian Court established under the Armed Forces Act 1976;
- detained under the deportation provisions of the Immigration Act 1971;
- detained under the Mental Health Act 1983, or the Mental Health (Scotland) Act 1984;
- imprisoned, detained or in custody (but not in custody under open arrest for the purposes of Queen's Regulations) for more than 48 hours under the Army Act 1955, the Air Force Act 1955 or the Naval Discipline Act 1957.[34]

The individual should still be treated as detained if temporarily discharged or temporarily released under the Prison Act 1952, or the Prisons (Scotland) Act 1989. A person detained for non-payment of the council tax in England or Wales or non-payment of a fine is not treated as detained for the purpose of a discount.[35]

The severely mentally impaired

For council tax purposes someone is considered severely mentally impaired if s/he has a severe impairment of intelligence and social functioning (however caused) which appears to be permanent.[36] This includes people who are severely mentally impaired as a result of a degenerative brain disorder such as Alzheimer's disease, a stroke or other forms of dementia. To count as severely mentally impaired the person concerned must have a certificate of confirmation from a registered medical practitioner. The British Medical Association has advised its members that no charge should be made for the issuing of such certificates. Practice Note No. 2, p24, advises that certificates of severe mental impairment issued before the introduction of council tax are acceptable provided that they do not include any condition that they will only be used for some other purpose, for instance, exemption from the community charge.

In addition, to qualify for the disregard the person must be entitled to (though not necessarily in receipt of) one of the following benefits:

- an invalidity pension (IVP); *or*
- an attendance allowance (AA); *or*
- a severe disablement allowance (SDA); *or*
- the highest or middle rate care component of a disability living allowance (DLA); *or*
- an increase in the rate of disablement pension for constant attendance; *or*

- a disability working allowance (DWA) – but only if this is because of the prior receipt of IVP or SDA (or a corresponding Northern Ireland benefit); *or*
- unemployability supplement; *or*
- a constant attendance allowance payable under the industrial injuries or war pension schemes; *or*
- an unemployability allowance payable under the industrial injuries or war pension schemes.

Hospital patients

If someone has a short stay in hospital it has no effect on council tax liability or the amount of tax that must be paid. If the patient has, or is likely to be, in a hospital for so long that s/he can no longer be considered to be solely or even mainly resident in the home then that person should be ignored for the purpose of a discount. A dwelling left empty by someone who is solely or mainly resident in hospital is exempt from the council tax (Chapter 5).

Most hospitals are subject to non-domestic rates but some types of long-stay hospitals can be considered dwellings for council tax purposes. Patients who are solely or mainly resident in such a hospital are disregarded for the purposes of a discount.[37] In this context, and for the purpose of exemptions, a 'hospital' means:

- an NHS hospital including any NHS Trust hospital; *and*
- a military, air force or naval unit or establishment at or in which medical or surgical treatment is provided for persons subject to military law, air force law or the Naval Discipline Act 1957.[38]

Persons in residential care/nursing homes, Scottish private hospitals and hostels providing a high level of care

The owners, rather than the residents, of these types of accommodation are liable for the council tax (Chapter 6). The owners of such dwellings may be eligible for a disability reduction (see Chapter 7). In addition, a person solely or mainly resident in such accommodation is disregarded for the purposes of a discount if receiving care or treatment (or both) in the home or hostel. Persons in equivalent accommodation in England, Wales and Scotland are discounted.[39] If such persons have left their own home empty it may be exempt from the council tax (Chapter 5).

Nursing homes, etc.

The different types of dwelling are defined as follows:

- a nursing home in England and Wales is anything which is registered as such with the health authority, or exempt from registration, under the Registered Homes Act 1984 and in Scotland is anything which must be registered or is exempt from registration under the Nursing Homes Registration (Scotland) Act 1938;[40]
- a 'mental nursing home' in England and Wales must be registered with the health authority under the Registered Homes Act 1984;[41]
- a 'private hospital' in Scotland is one that must be registered under section 12 (registration of private hospitals) of the Mental Health (Scotland) Act 1984.[42]

Residential care homes

In England and Wales a 'residential care home' is either:

- a dwelling which must be registered with the local social service authority under Part I of the Registered Homes Act 1984 unless it is exempt; *or*
- a dwelling in which residential accommodation is provided under section 21 of the National Assistance Act 1948, or run by the Abbeyfield Society, or an affiliated body.[43]

In Scotland a 'residential care home' is:

- a residential establishment provided and maintained by a local authority in respect of their functions under section 13B (provision of care and after-care) of the Social Work (Scotland) Act 1968; *or*
- a residential establishment to which Part IV of the said Act of 1968 applies; *or*
- residential accommodation provided and maintained by a local authority under section 7 (functions of local authorities) of the Mental Health (Scotland) Act 1984; [44]

where the sole or main function of the establishment or accommodation is to provide personal care or support, combined with board, to persons who are solely or mainly resident in the establishment or accommodation.

Hostels

In England and Wales hostels refers to bail and probation hostels approved under section 49(1) of the Powers of Criminal Courts Act 1973. It also refers to dwellings that are not a residential care home, nursing home or mental nursing home, but which provide:

- mainly communal residential accommodation; *and*
- personal care for people who need it because of old age,

disablement, past or present alcohol or drug dependence, or past or present mental disorder.[45]

A 'hostel' in Scotland is an establishment in which residential accommodation is provided and where the sole or main function of the establishment is to provide personal care or support to people who have their sole or main residence in the establishment. 'Personal care' includes the provision of appropriate help with physical and social needs and 'support' refers to counselling or other help provided as part of a planned programme of care. To qualify the hostel must be:

* managed by a registered housing association or a voluntary organisation within the meaning of section 94(1) of the Social Work (Scotland) Act 1968; *or*
* operated other than on a commercial basis and in respect of which funds are provided wholly or in part by a government department or agency or a local authority.[46]

Carer

A carer is disregarded for the purpose of a discount if s/he is providing care or support (or both) to another person in one of three circumstances.[47] These are that:

1. the carer is providing care on behalf of an official or charitable body;
2. the carer is employed by the person being cared for and introduced by a charitable body;
3. the person being cared for is in receipt of certain benefits.

In each case additional conditions must be met before the carer can be disregarded.

In the first instance the carer must be:

* providing the care or support in question on behalf of a local authority, the Common Council of the City of London; the Council of the Isles of Scilly; a government department; or a charitable body; *and*
* resident in premises provided by, or on behalf of that organisation, so that the best care can be provided; *and*
* engaged or employed for at least 24 hours a week; *and*
* in receipt under her/his engagement or employment of not more than £30 remuneration a week.

In the second instance the last two conditions are the same but the carer must be:

- employed to provide care or support by the person who needs the care; *and*
- introduced to that person by a charitable body; *and*
- resident in premises provided by, or on behalf of, the person being cared for to enable the best care to be provided.

In the third instance the carer must be:

- resident in the same dwelling as the person being cared for;
- providing that care for at least 35 hours a week on average; *and*
- not a partner of the opposite sex, or if the person needing care is a child under 18, not the child's parent.

In addition, in this third instance the person being cared for must be in receipt of (not just entitled to):

- a higher rate attendance allowance (AA); *or*
- the highest rate of the care component of a disability living allowance (DLA); *or*
- an increase in the rate of a disablement pension under section 104 of the Social Security Contributions and Benefits Act 1992; *or*
- an increase in a constant attendance allowance under the industrial injuries or war pensions scheme.

A dwelling left empty by a carer is exempt whether or not the carer meets any of the above definitions. A dwelling left empty by someone who has moved to receive care is also exempt (Chapter 5).

Members of international headquarters and defence organisations

A person is disregarded for discount purposes if s/he is a member or a dependant of a member of certain international headquarters or defence organisations. The headquarters and defence organisations in question are the subject of an order in council under section 1 of the International and Defence Organisations Act 1964.[48]

Members of visiting forces

Members of visiting forces and any of their dependants who are neither British citizens nor ordinarily resident in the United Kingdom are disregarded for the purposes of a discount.[49]

Members of religious communities

A person is a member of a religious community if:

- the principal occupation of the community consists of prayer, contemplation, education, the relief of suffering, or any combination of these; *and*
- s/he has no income or capital of her/his own and is dependent on the community to provide for her/his material needs.[50]

In considering whether or not the individual has any income the authority should disregard any pension or pensions from former employment.

The owner rather than the residents is liable for the tax on dwellings occupied by religious communities (Chapter 6).

Residents in certain hostels, night shelters, etc.

In England and Wales a person is disregarded for the purposes of discount if her or his sole or main residence is in a dwelling such as those run by the Salvation Army or Church Army for people of no fixed abode and no settled way of life. Most of the accommodation must be communal, ie not be sub-divided into self-contained units and most agreements to occupy the accommodation must be under licences which do not constitute tenancies. The disregard applies to resident staff as well as users so long as the accommodation is predominantly provided for those with no fixed abode on the terms and conditions specified.

How are discounts obtained?

Before calculating the council tax liability of any dwelling in its area an authority should take reasonable steps to ascertain whether any discount should be granted.[51] Initially many authorities used their community charge and other records to identify when a discount applied. Many also sent out questionnaires to all households.

Where the authority has reason to believe that a discount applies this should be assumed in the calculation of the council tax liability for the dwelling.[52] Practice Note No. 2 (para 55) points out that an authority may have reason to believe that a discount applies (and hence may be required to apply one) even if it does not have conclusive evidence.

Applications for discounts

If the authority has not granted a discount then the liable person may write to it requesting the discount. Any relevant evidence that supports the request should be included. In the case of a student a student's certificate may prove useful but is not necessary. In the case of someone who is severely mentally impaired a certificate from a GP is required. Practice Note No. 2 (para 59) reminds authorities that anyone who presents information which they know to be false in order to reduce their council tax bill may be subject to prosecution for obtaining a pecuniary advantage by deception. It advises authorities to pass any evidence of such deception to the police.

Backdating discounts

Many authorities have 'claim' forms for council tax discounts. While filling in such a form may speed up the award of a discount the granting of a discount is not dependent upon a 'claim'. Authorities must therefore grant discounts for a past period if the appropriate conditions were met. Unlike the provisions for backdating most social security benefits there is no requirement for 'good cause' to be shown before a discount is backdated. Equally where a discount should not have been granted for a past period it may be withdrawn.

The duty to correct false assumptions

If a discount has been granted the authority must inform the liable person of that fact in writing normally on the tax bill. If that person, or any jointly liable person, has reason to believe that the discount should not have been awarded a letter must be written to the authority advising them of that belief within 21 days.[53] This obligation to inform the authority only arises before the end of the financial year following the financial year in respect of which the authority's assumption about the discount is made.[54]

Penalties

The authority has the discretion to impose a penalty of £50 on a liable person who fails to notify the authority of their belief that a discount should not have been granted.[55] An English or Welsh authority may quash such a penalty. A Scottish authority may revoke the imposition of such a penalty if the person upon whom it was imposed had a reasonable excuse for the failure.[56] Each time the authority repeats the request and the person fails to supply the information a further £200 penalty can be imposed.[57]

An appeal against the imposition of a penalty may be made (Chapter 13).[58] In England and Wales this is done by writing directly to the valuation tribunal. In Scotland an appeal can be made to the valuation appeal committee by writing to the authority. The authority should pass the appeal on to the committee. An appeal should be made within two months of the imposition of the penalty. If such an appeal has been made then the penalty need not be paid until the appeal has been decided.

How is an appeal made against a refusal to grant a discount?

If the authority refuses to grant an discount an appeal can be made by the aggrieved person writing to the authority.[59] There is no time limit for the making of such an appeal. The aggrieved person is someone who is liable to pay the tax if the dwelling were not exempt and also the owner if different. The appeal letter should give the reasons why the property should be exempt. The authority has two months in which to answer.[60]

If an exemption is not granted, or if the authority fails to answer within two months of receipt of the appeal, a further appeal can be made (Chapter 13).[61] In England and Wales this is done by writing directly to the valuation tribunal. In Scotland a further appeal is made by writing again to the authority. The authority should pass the appeal on to the secretary of the relevant local valuation appeal committee. In England and Wales this must normally be done within two months of the date the authority notified the aggrieved person of its decision, or within four months of the date when the initial representation was made if the authority has not responded. The president of the tribunal has the power to allow an out-of-time appeal where the aggrieved person has failed to meet the appropriate time limit for reasons beyond her/his control. In Scotland the appeal must be made within four months of the date on which the grievance was first raised with the authority in writing. There is no power to consider an out-of-time appeal. The authority may enforce payment of the original bill while the appeal is outstanding (Chapter 12).

CHAPTER NINE

Transitional reduction

This chapter explains:

- which dwellings qualify for a transitional reduction;
- who is eligible to receive a transitional reduction;
- how the amount of the transitional reduction is worked out;
- the changes of circumstance that lead to a change in a transitional reduction; *and*
- an aggrieved person's appeal rights.

Transitional reduction schemes exist in England and Scotland but not Wales.[1] The aim of the scheme is to limit the increase that some households face as a result of the transition from the community charge to the council tax. It does not cover the council water charge in Scotland.

A transitional reduction may be granted in addition to a disability reduction (Chapter 7), a discount (Chapter 8) or CTB (Chapter 10). It is worked out on the basis of a council tax liability on 1 April 1993 after any disability reduction or discount granted for that date but ignoring any CTB entitlement. CTB is worked out on the council tax payable after any transitional reduction has been granted.

Which dwellings qualify for a transitional reduction?

The reduction is best thought of as belonging to the dwelling rather than the liable person. A qualifying dwelling is one which at the end of the day on 31 March 1993 was someone's sole or main residence.[2] This includes dwellings which were:

- the sole or main residence of one or more persons who were subject to the community charge; *or*
- subject to the collective community charge; *or*
- the sole or main residence of one or more persons aged under 18 only; *or*
- the sole or main residence of one or more persons who were exempt from the community charge.

Dwellings which were no one's sole or main residence at the end of 31 March 1993 never qualify for a transitional reduction. Also, new dwellings completed after 31 March 1993 are not 'qualifying dwellings' and no transitional reduction can be granted on them. Additionally in Scotland, but not England, a dwelling which is exempt (Chapter 5) from the council tax on 1 April 1993 does not qualify.[3]

Who is eligible for a transitional reduction?

A person is eligible for a transitional reduction on a particular day if s/he is:

- liable to pay an amount of council tax in respect of a qualifying dwelling; *and*
- someone, not necessarily the liable person, who has her/his sole or main residence in the dwelling.[4]

Given the above eligibility rules someone may 'inherit' or lose a transitional reduction if s/he moves home. A liable person who is not resident in a property, eg a landlord of a multi-occupied property, may still be eligible so long as another person is resident.

How is a transitional reduction worked out?

In general terms the scheme can be said to compensate those households that face a significant increase in their local tax payments as a result of the transition from community charge to council tax by comparing:

- the amount of community charge payable by people in the dwelling (but in Scotland excluding any community water charge) on 31 March 1993;

with

- the amount of council tax payable on the dwelling (but in Scotland excluding council water charge) on 1 April 1993;

and limiting that increase to a certain amount, or threshold figure, depending upon the dwelling's valuation band.

Exhibit 9.1   Working out a transitional reduction

Notional rather than actual figures are used – see the main text

Daily transitional reduction = $\dfrac{CT - (CC + TF)}{D}$

Where:

CT   is the annual council tax payable on 1 April 1993;
CC   is the annual community charge payable on 31 March 1993;
TF   is the annual threshold figure, ie the maximum increase that the liable person should have to pay for a dwelling in a particular valuation band as a result of the transition from the community charge to the council tax; *and*

D is the number of days in the financial year (ie 365 or 366).

Why isn't the increase always limited to the threshold figure?

In practice it is very rare for any increase in costs due to the introduction of the council tax to be limited to the appropriate threshold figure. This is because notional rather than actual figures are used in the calculation.

The council tax figure

In England the annual council tax figure used in the calculation of the transitional reduction is whichever is the lower of:

● the scheme council tax; *and*
● the set council tax for the relevant year applicable to the dwelling.

The scheme council tax is one set by the government in relation to the authority and the valuation band applicable to the dwelling on 1 April 1993.[5] The set council tax is the amount set for the relevant year by the authority in relation to the valuation band and area (or part) applicable to the dwelling.[6]

In Scotland the figure used is whichever is the lower of:

● the adjusted council tax calculated according to rules set by government; *and*

- the sum of the council taxes set by the district and regional council, or the islands' council tax.[7]

In all cases the transitional reduction is based on the council tax liability after any actual discounts or disability reduction that applied on 1 April 1993 but prior to the award of any CTB.

The community charge figure

CC is the annual community charge in respect of the dwelling and is calculated as follows:

- in England the scheme charge set by the government but derived from the authority's average personal community charge in 1992/93 (averaging out the effects of any parish precepts);[8] *or*
- in Scotland the islands council's personal community charge or the aggregate of the regional and district council's personal community charges;[9]
- multiplied by the number of chargepayers in the dwelling either subject to a personal community charge or liable to make collective community charge contributions;

  minus

- any relief under the community charge reduction scheme; *and*
- any 80 per cent student relief awarded to people in the dwelling.

The calculation assumes that as far as the community charge reduction and student relief are concerned the circumstances of an individual on 31 March 1993 had applied throughout 1992/93. Those authorities which issued council tax bills before the end of March must have made some errors.

The threshold figure

The threshold figure is an amount set by government. It is supposed to represent the maximum increase that would have to be paid if the authority had set a reasonable council tax. Different fixed amounts apply to different valuation bands as Exhibit 9.2 illustrates.[10] Where a person was eligible on 1 April 1993 for a reduction for disability in respect of the qualifying dwelling, the fixed amount is the one for the alternative valuation band that applies in such cases (Chapter 7).[11]

Daily transitional reduction

The amount arrived at by subtracting (CC + TF) from CT is divided by D (the number of days in the financial year). This enables the

Exhibit 9.2   Transitional relief thresholds: England and Scotland

Valuation band	Maximum increase
A	£1.75 a week or £91 a year
B	£2.00 a week or £104 a year
C	£2.25 a week or £117 a year
D	£2.50 a week or £130 a year
E	£2.75 a week or £143 a year
F	£3.00 a week or £156 a year
G	£3.25 a week or £169 a year
H	£3.50 a week or £182 a year

eligible person's reduced liability on a day to be calculated and part-year reductions to be properly identified. Where $(CC + TF)$ is greater than CT no reduction is granted. Where the amount of the reduction is greater than the tax payable the liability is nil. Otherwise the resulting amount is granted as a transitional reduction.

Example

Two adults live in a house. One is the owner, the other a lodger.

The combined community charge payable by the two adults in the dwelling on 31 March 1993 and after any community charge transitional relief or student reduction (CC) was £450.

The home is in band D. The actual amount that must be paid in council tax is £650 which is £50 above the government's council tax figure of £600 (CT).

The threshold figure (TF) for a band D property is £130.

$$\text{Transitional reduction} = \frac{CT - (CC + TF)}{D}$$

ie £600 — (450 + 130) ÷ 365 = £0.0548 a day or £20 a year.

The liable owner's initial bill should be £630, ie the actual amount payable (£650) minus the transitional reduction of £20.

Despite the fact that the threshold figure on this dwelling is £130 the actual increase that must be paid over the community charges that were payable in the dwelling is £180 a year. In Scotland council water charge must be paid as well.

Will the transitional reduction change?

The amount of the transitional reduction remains the same except:

- where the information on the state of affairs on 31 March 1993 and/or 1 April 1993 is found to have been incorrect and must be amended;
- where changes in entitlement to a disability reduction or discount are backdated to 1 April 1993;
- where the valuation banding of a dwelling is altered;
- where the set tax for a year is lower than the scheme council tax and differs from that set for 1993/94; *and*
- to phase the transitional reduction out over future years.

The transitional reduction is suspended for any day that the dwelling is exempt from the charge or no one is solely or mainly resident in the dwelling. Once a qualifying dwelling is no longer exempt or once it becomes someone's sole or main residence again the original daily rate of transitional reduction should be re-applied.

The amount of the transitional reduction does not change if there are changes in:

- the liable person;
- the number of liable persons;
- the number of occupants;
- entitlement to a disability reduction; *or*
- discount entitlement.

For example the grant of a disability reduction or a discount commencing after 1 April 1993 should not alter the amount of the transitional reduction.

Local authority boundary changes

In England where, as a result of local government boundary changes, a qualifying dwelling falls within another authority's area, any council tax reduction should be re-calculated from that time on the basis of the scheme community charge of the old authority and the scheme or set council tax of the new authority.[12] There are no specific provisions in the regulations relating to impending boundary changes in Scotland.

How is a transitional reduction obtained?

No claim need be made for a transitional reduction. It should be granted automatically by the authority to an eligible person where the calculation shows her or him to be eligible for an amount.

In considering whether someone is entitled to a transitional reduction the authority may write to the person in question requesting information to assist. That person should be given at least 21 days in which to reply.[13] If a transitional reduction has been granted it should be shown on the council tax bill.

Backdating a transitional reduction

Where the authority, or the review board (see below), later decide that a transitional reduction should have been granted it should be granted from 1 April 1993 at the appropriate level for the year or years in question. Unlike the provisions for backdating most social security benefits there is no requirement for anyone to show 'good cause' for any backdating of a transitional reduction.

Obtaining an explanation of the authority's decisions

Any person affected by an authority's decision in relation to a transitional reduction may request the authority to provide a written statement of its decision and the reasons for it. The authority must date the statement and send it out within 14 days of the date it is requested or as soon as is reasonably practicable thereafter.[14]

How is an appeal made against a refusal to grant a transitional reduction?

Any person aggrieved by the authority's decision on a transitional reduction may appeal to its CTB review board rather than a valuation tribunal or valuation assessment committee. The aggrieved person (the appellant) must write an appeal letter to the authority.[15] There is no time limit in which such appeals need to be made.

The authority does not have to arrange a review board within six weeks of receiving the request from the appellant, as it would have to with a CTB appeal. It should, however, as a matter of good practice, deal with such appeals in a timely manner. Normally at least ten days' notice should be given of the date of the hearing though it may go ahead with less notice if all the parties agree.

The review board normally consists of at least three elected members of the authority with one member taking the chair. The hearing may go ahead with only two board members present if the authority and the aggrieved person agree. The review board is expected to take an independent stance. Either the authority or the aggrieved person may apply in writing to the chair requesting a postponement of the hearing. It is for the chair to decide whether such a postponement should be granted. If either party fails to appear at the hearing, having indicated that they would be present, the review board may decide to go ahead with the hearing or take such other course of action, eg postponement, as it thinks proper.[16]

The procedures to be followed at the hearing are for the chair to determine subject to the rules of natural justice. Both the authority and the aggrieved person have the right:

- to make written representations to the review board;
- to attend the hearing;
- to be heard at the hearing;
- to be represented by someone;
- to call persons to give evidence and to put questions to any one who gives evidence.

The chair must record the review board's decision in writing and include the reasons for its decision and any findings of fact. The decision note should be sent to the aggrieved person and the authority within seven days of the hearing or as soon as reasonably practicable after that.

The authority has the power to meet the travel expenses of the aggrieved person and one other person accompanying or representing the aggrieved person.

The authority must comply with the review board's decision.[17] Unlike CTB cases there is no provision for the setting aside of a review board's decision on a transitional reduction. An application may, however, be made for judicial review if the review board has made an error in law.

CHAPTER TEN

Council tax benefit (CTB)

This chapter explains:

- the two forms of CTB;
- who can claim main CTB and second adult rebate;
- how the two forms of CTB are worked out;
- how a claim is made; *and*
- how an appeal is made against the authority's determinations on CTB.

CTB is a benefit administered by authorities to assist certain liable persons with their council tax payments. It operates throughout Great Britain from 1 April 1993. CTB has many of the same features as the housing benefit scheme. In appropriate cases it is able to meet up to 100 per cent of an individual's council tax liability. It does not cover the council water charge in Scotland. The maximum take-up of CTB not only assists low income households with their council tax payments, it also reduces the authority's collection costs and reduces the scope for council tax arrears.

Legal and other sources

The primary legislation governing the CTB scheme is contained in the:

- Social Security Administration Act 1992 (as amended by the Local Government Finance Act 1992); *and*
- Social Security Contributions and Benefits Act 1992 (as amended by the Local Government Finance Act 1992).[1]

The detailed rules of the scheme are contained in SI 1992 No. 1814 The Council Tax Benefit (General) Regulations as amended by:

- SI 1993 No. 349 The Social Security Benefits Up-rating Order;
- SI 1993 No. 688 The Council Tax Benefit (General) Amendment Regulations;
- SI 1993 No. 963 The Social Security Benefits (Miscellaneous

Amendments) No. 2 Regulations;

- SI 1993 No. 1150 The Income-Related Benefits Schemes (Miscellaneous Amendments) (No. 2) Regulations;
- SI 1993 No. 1249 The Income-Related Benefits Schemes and Social Security (Recoupment) Amendment Regulations.

The special arrangements to ease the introduction of the new scheme are contained in SI 1992 No. 1909 The Council Tax Benefit (Transitional) Order.

In addition to the DoE Practice Note on CTB (Appendix 3) the DSS have issued a *Housing Benefit and Council Tax Benefit Guidance Manual* that provides authorities with advice on the scheme. It is available from HMSO. A detailed explanation of the workings of the scheme may be found in this author's and John Zebedee's *Housing Benefit and Council Tax Guide* 1993–94 available from the Child Poverty Action Group.

What are the different forms of CTB?

CTB takes two forms:

- main CTB; *and*
- alternative maximum CTB – more commonly referred to as second adult rebate.

Main CTB is based on the claimant's council tax liability and her/his (and any partner's and dependants') assumed needs and resources.

Second adult rebate is a form of CTB but it is not based on the claimant's needs or resources. Rather it is based on the circumstances of certain other adults (second adults) living with the claimant.

Who is eligible for main CTB?

For someone to be entitled to main CTB on any day s/he must be:

- liable to pay council tax in respect of a dwelling; *and*
- a resident of that dwelling.[2]

Both 'dwelling' and 'resident' in the CTB rules have the same meaning as for council tax purposes (Chapter 6).[3]

The following people are not entitled to CTB:

- owners, not resident in the dwelling, or those whose main residence is elsewhere (eg second home owners);[4]

- people under the age of 18;[5] *and*
- full-time students, except 'protected' students.[6]

Full-time students are able to claim second adult rebate if they satisfy the normal qualifying conditions for that form of the benefit (see below).[7] The definition of a student for CTB purposes is different from that for council tax purposes and mirrors the provision for housing benefit. For CTB a student is simply someone who is attending a course of study at an educational establishment. Once a course has started a person counts as a student until:

- the last day of the course (ie the end of the final academic term of the course); *or*
- until she or he abandons, or is dismissed, from it.[8]

'Full-time' is not defined for CTB purposes except that it includes a student on a sandwich course.[9] Benefit authorities are not bound by the more precise definitions used for the purposes of awarding status discounts to students under the council tax scheme.

Protected students

The 'protected' students potentially entitled to main CTB are:

- those receiving income support;
- those entitled to:
  - the lone parent premium;
  - one of the pensioner premiums (ie aged 60 or more);
  - the disability or severe disability premium;
- those with partners who are also full-time students if either partner is treated as responsible for a child or young person (ie someone under 19 for whom child benefit is payable);
- those who are single but fostering a child or young person formally placed with them by a local authority or voluntary agency;
- those aged under 19 not in higher education (ie in a course that is not higher than A level);
- those who are deaf students satisfying the conditions for a mandatory or discretionary addition to their grant because of their deafness.[10]

Main CTB may, however, be claimed by:

- part-time students;
- the non-student partner of a full-time student for the couple's council tax liability;

- employment trainees in receipt of a training allowance;
- people on other training courses which do not take place at an educational establishment (eg student nurses following hospital-based training).

Examples

Two brothers are the joint owners of the dwelling in which they live. The older brother is a full-time student. He is disregarded for the purpose of a council tax discount (Chapter 8). The younger brother is in low-paid employment.

Their sister also lives with them. She is unemployed. For the last six months they have also put up their sister's friend – a lone parent on income support and with a child aged two.

In these circumstances only the younger brother/joint owner is eligible for main CTB. While the sister and her friend are also resident in the dwelling neither is liable for the tax as the two joint owners are resident and consequently neither is eligible for CTB. The older brother is jointly liable but as a full-time student who does not fall into a protected group he is not eligible for main CTB (though he is eligible for second adult rebate – see below).

If the younger brother went to live elsewhere the older student brother would be solely liable for the council tax but no one in the dwelling would be eligible to receive main CTB.

If the older brother were to live with his sister's friend 'as husband and wife' in the dwelling his partner would become jointly liable for the council tax. She could claim main CTB as the non-student partner though it would be based on the combined needs and resources of the claimant and her student partner.

How is CTB worked out?

Maximum benefit

The starting point for all main CTB calculations is the claimant's 'maximum benefit' figure. 'Maximum benefit' consists of:

- 100 per cent of the net (apportioned) weekly council tax liability;

MINUS

- the total of any (apportioned) non-dependant deductions.[11]

Income support claimants

Where the claimant is entitled to IS her/his main CTB entitlement equals the maximum CTB figure.

Example

A single tenant lives alone. He is liable for a weekly council tax of £10. He is also in receipt of income support. His weekly CTB entitlement is £10.

Non-income support claimant

Where the claimant is not on IS the authority needs to assess her/his:

- capital such as money in a bank account or property;
- earned and unearned income; *and*
- needs – as represented by the claimant's applicable amount.

Where an non-income support claimant and any partner have capital of more than £16,000 there is no entitlement to main CTB but the claimant may be entitled to second adult rebate. Certain capital, however, such as the claimant's home and personal possessions are disregarded as for housing benefit.

The claimant's assessed income for CTB purposes is compared with the appropriate applicable amount (a figure set each year by central government to reflect the claimant's weekly needs). If the claimant's net income for benefit purposes is less than, or equal to, the appropriate applicable amount then the CTB entitlement equals the maximum benefit figure. If the claimant's net income for benefit purposes exceeds her/his applicable amount the maximum CTB figure is reduced by 20 per cent of the excess income figure.[12]

Example

A single tenant lives alone. He is liable for a weekly council tax of £10. Therefore the maximum council tax benefit is £10. The claimant's income that counts for benefit purposes exceeds his applicable amount by £20. The maximum CTB figure is reduced by £4, ie 20 per cent of the £20 excess income. Consequently his weekly main CTB entitlement is £6.

Additional main CTB in exceptional circumstances

The authority may increase the amount of main CTB allowed up to 100 per cent of the council tax liability for CTB purposes before any non-dependant deductions are made if the authority considers the claimant's circumstances are exceptional.[13]

The council tax used to work out main CTB

The council tax liability for main CTB purposes is that which remains after any of the following that apply have been granted:

- a disability reduction (Chapter 7);
- discounts (Chapter 8); *and*
- any transitional reduction (Chapter 9).[14]

The delayed award of a disability reduction, a discount or a reduction under the council tax reduction scheme where CTB has previously been awarded using the higher liability gives rise to a recoverable CTB overpayment.[15]

The annual net council tax liability is converted to a weekly figure by dividing the annual figure by the number of days in the financial year (365 or 366) to find the daily council tax. Then multiply by seven to give the weekly figure used in the calculation.

Where the authority awards a reduction for a lump sum payment at the beginning of the financial year (Chapter 11) CTB is calculated on the basis of the council tax liability disregarding any such reduction.[16] Where the council tax bill has been increased to recover an overpayment of council tax any such increase is ignored for the purpose of working out CTB.[17] The council tax liability for the purpose of calculating second adult rebate differs (see below).

Apportionment of council tax liability between liable residents for main CTB purposes

Where a claimant is jointly liable for council tax in respect of a dwelling (except where liability is shared *only* with a partner) the annual council tax liability is divided by the number of persons who are jointly liable in order to arrive at the apportioned figure used for CTB purposes.[18] This rule is different from, and simpler than, the rule relating to the apportionment of rent for housing benefit purposes. With that benefit the authority must decide the rent fairly attributable to each person taking into account the number of people making payments, the proportion of rent paid by each and any other relevant factors – such as the number of rooms each occupies, etc.

Examples

Two women own and reside in a house. They are both jointly liable for the annual council tax of £600 on the dwelling.

One of the women loses her job and claims CTB. She is only eligible for main CTB on her share of the council tax, consequently the annual council tax liability (£600) is divided by the number of persons (2) who are jointly liable for the tax to arrive at the claimant's council tax liability for CTB purposes, ie £300.

If one of the women had a male partner, however, he would be jointly liable by virtue of that relationship. There would be three persons jointly liable in the dwelling. If the woman without a partner were to apply for CTB, her apportioned annual liability for CTB purposes would be £200, ie £600 ÷ 3.

If either partner in the couple were to apply for CTB for the couple, their apportioned annual liability for main CTB purposes would be £400, ie (£600 ÷ 3) × 2.

This method of apportionment of council tax for CTB purposes gives rise to a particular problem. A person who is jointly liable can be pursued for the full amount of the tax due on the dwelling (Chapter 12) while receiving benefit only on her/his 'share' of the joint liability.

Non-dependants

The claimant's maximum CTB is reduced where certain people, known as non-dependants, normally reside with the claimant.[19] Non-dependants typically include grown-up sons and daughters residing with the claimant. Certain people, however, do not count as non-dependants including:

- any person who, with the claimant, is jointly liable to pay the council tax (Chapter 6);
- any person who is liable to make payments on a commercial basis to the claimant, or the claimant's partner, in respect of the occupation of the dwelling, eg a boarder, or tenant but not someone who is a close relative or where the agreement is on other than a commercial basis or in most cases where it has been created to take advantage of the CTB scheme;
- a person who lives with the claimant:
  - in order to care for the claimant or the claimant's partner, *and*
  - who is engaged by a charitable or voluntary body (other than

a public or local authority) which makes a charge to the claimant or partner for the service provided;
- any member of the claimant's family for benefit purposes, ie partner and dependants;
- a child or young person (someone under 18 for whom child benefit is payable) who is:
  - living with the claimant, but
  - not a member of the claimant's family for CTB purposes, eg a foster child.[20]

Non-dependant deductions

Non-dependant deductions are not related to what the non-dependant actually pays. They are fixed amounts which apply even if the non-dependant pays the claimant nothing at all. Council tax arrears often develop where the claimant does not receive a contribution from the non-dependant. Exhibit 10.1 summarises the non-dependant deductions that apply in 1993–94.[21]

Exhibit 10.1 Non-dependant deductions: (1993–94)	
Non-dependants in remunerative work	
• with gross income of £105 +	£2
• with gross income below £104.99	£1
Non-dependants not in remunerative work	£1

Remunerative work is work of 16 hours or more per week carried out for payment, or the expectation of payment.[22] Gross income includes both earned and unearned income but any disability living allowance and attendance allowance are disregarded.

Only one non-dependant deduction is made for a non-dependant couple. Where, except for this rule, different amounts would be deducted for each partner as individuals, the highest amount is always made on behalf of the couple. However, it is the couple's joint gross income which always counts when calculating the level of deduction where either, or both, of them are in remunerative work. Where the non-dependant is the non-dependant of two or more liable persons, the non-dependant deduction is split equally between them. The other liable person does not have to be claiming CTB to cause the deduction to be apportioned.[23]

Examples

The claimant is a joint tenant of a dwelling with his partner. Their son aged 25 works 21 hours a week and earns £80 a week gross. A non-dependant deduction of £1 is made from the claimant's weekly net council tax liability for the purpose of calculating maximum CTB.

The son marries and the couple live in the claimant's household. The son's partner has a gross weekly income of £85 a week. Only one non-dependant deduction is made but it is based on the couple's combined gross income. A £2 deduction is made from the claimant's net weekly council tax liability for the purpose of calculating the claimant's maximum CTB because the non-dependants' combined gross income is over £104.99 a week.

No non-dependant deductions for certain claimants

No non-dependant deductions are made where the claimant or partner is:

- registered as blind or, having been registered, has regained her or his eyesight within the last 28 weeks; or
- receiving in respect of her/himself:
  - the care component of the disability living allowance, or
  - an attendance allowance.[24]

Example

The claimant looks after her pensioner husband who receives the care component of the disability living allowance. Their three sons who are all working full time and earning over £650 each a week are aged 22, 24 and 26. No non-dependant deduction is made.

No deduction for certain non-dependants

No deductions are made for any non-dependant who:

- resides with the claimant if it appears to the authority that her or his normal home is elsewhere; or
- is in receipt of a youth training allowance; or
- is a full-time student for CTB purposes; or
- is on income support; or
- is aged under 18; or
- is not residing with the claimant because the individual has been an NHS patient for a period in excess of six weeks (two stays in hospital are added together for the purpose of counting the six

weeks' period if the break between them is four weeks or less); *or*

- is a person who is disregarded for the purpose of a council tax discount except where that person counts as a student for the purpose of the discount (Chapter 8) but no deduction is made for full-time students – see above.[25]

Income

Income includes both earned and unearned income.[26] The claimant's (and any partner's) net earned income is taken into account. The net earned income is worked out by deducting income tax, class 1 national insurance contributions and 50 per cent of any contributions towards a pension from the gross earnings' figure. Certain earned income is disregarded. The main earned income disregards are:

- £25 for lone parents;
- £15 if the claimant's applicable amount includes a disability, severe disability or carer premium;
- £10 for couples; *and*
- £5 for single claimants.[27]

Most unearned income such as occupational pensions and certain benefits are taken into account but certain types of unearned income are disregarded in full or in part.[28] Additionally the authority may pass a resolution modifying the national CTB scheme so that when calculating the claimant's net weekly income, the £10 a week disregard that normally applies to a war disablement pension, or a war widow's pension, is increased by any amount up to 100 per cent.[29]

Where the claimant and any partner has capital that counts for CTB purposes of between £3,000 and £16,000 it is assumed to provide the claimant with £1 a week in income for each £250 or part thereof between £3,000 and £16,000.[30]

Applicable amounts

The claimant's weekly financial needs for CTB purposes are represented by way of applicable amounts (Exhibit 10.2). These are set each year by central government. The applicable amount is made up of:

- personal allowances – which vary according to the age of the claimant and any married or unmarried partner; *and*
- dependant's allowances for each child or young person varying according to age; *and*
- premiums – to meet the additional needs of specific groups (Exhibit 10.3).[31]

Exhibit 10.2 Applicable amounts 1993–94

Personal allowances
Single claimant

aged under 25	£34.80
aged 25 or over	£44.00
Lone parent aged 18 or over	£44.00
Couple at least one aged 18 +	£69.00

Dependant's allowances
For each child or young person who does not have capital that counts for main CTB purposes over £3,000

aged under 11	£15.05
aged 11 to 15 inclusive	£22.15
aged 16 or 17	£26.45
aged 18	£34.80

Premiums
Any of the following premiums that apply are used

Family	£9.65
Each disabled child	£18.45
Severe disability	
single claimant or lone parent	£33.70
couple (only one satisfies conditions)	£33.70
couple (both satisfy conditions)	£67.40

Only the highest of the following premiums that apply is used

Lone parent	£10.95
Pensioner (60–74)	
single claimant/lone parent	£17.30
couple	£26.25
Enhanced pensioner (75–80)	
single claimant/lone parent	£19.30
couple	£29.00
Higher pensioner (80 +)	
single claimant/lone parent	£23.55
couple	£33.70
Disability premium	
single claimant/lone parent	£18.45
couple	£26.45
Carer's premium	£11.95

Exhibit 10.3   Premiums and main conditions

Premium	Main conditions
Family	Claimant is responsible for a child or young person.
Lone parent	Claimant has no partner and is responsible for a child or young person.
Disabled child	Child or young person does not have capital over £3,000 and receives disability living allowance or is registered blind.
Disability	Claimant or partner receives an attendance or mobility supplement, invalidity pension, attendance, disability living, disability working, or severe disablement allowance; or registered blind; or has (an allowance for) an invalid vehicle or the claimant has been incapable of work due to sickness or disability for 28 weeks.
Severe disability	Claimant receives an attendance allowance or the higher or middle rate care component of the disability living allowance and no one receives invalid care allowance to look after her/him and no adult in the household is able to care for the claimant. The couple rate is only payable if the above applies to both the claimant and partner.
Pensioner	Claimant or partner aged 60 or over.
Enhanced pensioner	Claimant or partner aged 75 or over.
Higher pensioner	Claimant or partner aged 80 or over; or aged 60 or over and satisfies the condition for the disability premium.
Carer	Claimant or partner receives invalid care allowance or has claimed it on or after 1 October 1990 but could not be paid it because of receipt of another higher benefit. Couples can get a double premium if each partner satisfies one of these conditions.

Where a claimant lives with a member of the opposite sex with whom they are married or living together as husband and wife, the benefit claim is based on the combined needs (applicable amount) and resources (income and capital) of both partners.

In determining whether two unmarried persons of the opposite sex should be regarded as *living together as husband and wife*, social security caselaw requires the benefit authority to take account of the following factors:

- Do the couple share the same household?
- Is the relationship as stable as a marriage?
- Are the financial arrangements shared or separate?
- Is there a sexual relationship?
- Is there any shared responsibility for children?
- Do they present themselves as a couple in public?
- What are the stated intentions of both parties?

All of the above should be considered as a whole in reaching a conclusion.[31a] The presence, or absence, of an individual factor (apart from non-membership of the same household) cannot, by itself, be conclusive.

What is second adult rebate?

Second adult rebate is a form of CTB but the amount of benefit is based on the income of certain other adults that may live with the claimant. Second adult rebate is designed to deal with the anomaly that occurs where:

- the presence of at least one other adult in the dwelling (a second adult) deprives the liable person of a discount on her or his council tax bill;
- the second adult, because s/he is on income support or a low income, finds it difficult to make a contribution to the liable person's council tax bill;
- the second adult is ineligible for any assistance in making a contribution to the council tax bill either:
  - *directly* through main CTB because she or he is not a liable person, *or*
  - *indirectly* through HB on rent (which includes an element to meet the council tax) paid to the liable person (eg as a boarder) because s/he is not living in the household on a commercial basis.

The above situation may apply to more than one adult living with the claimant. In other words there may be a number of second adults in the claimant's household. It is, however, a liable person and not the second adult who is entitled to second adult rebate. Claimants with more than £16,000 capital or full-time students are not excluded from second adult rebate.

Who is entitled to second adult rebate?

A person is potentially entitled to second adult rebate if:

- s/he is liable to pay council tax in respect of a dwelling in which s/he is resident;
- there is at least one 'second adult' resident in the dwelling; *and*
- there is no other resident of the dwelling who is liable to pay rent to the claimant in respect of the dwelling (apart from someone who is disregarded for the purpose of a council tax discount – Chapter 8).

However, the DSS appears to take the view that this exception (ie the rule contained within box 6 of the flowchart) does not apply and that, in effect, the presence of *any* other resident paying rent to the claimant (ie answering 'yes' to the question in box 5 of the flowchart) disqualifies the claimant from a second adult rebate in all cases. Given that this is a contentious issue, both authorities and advisers may wish to refer directly to the (ambiguous) legislation on this point.[32]

Liable persons excluded from second adult rebate

Second adult rebate is not available in those cases where the claimant:

- lives with one or more other persons (including a partner) who is or are jointly liable for the council tax on the dwelling; *and*
- at least two of the liable persons are not disregarded for the purpose of a council tax discount (Chapter 8).[33]

The reason for these exclusions is that no discounts would have been awarded in such cases regardless of the additional presence of a second adult.

Who counts as a second adult?

A second adult is someone who resides with the claimant on a non-

Entitlement to second adult rebate

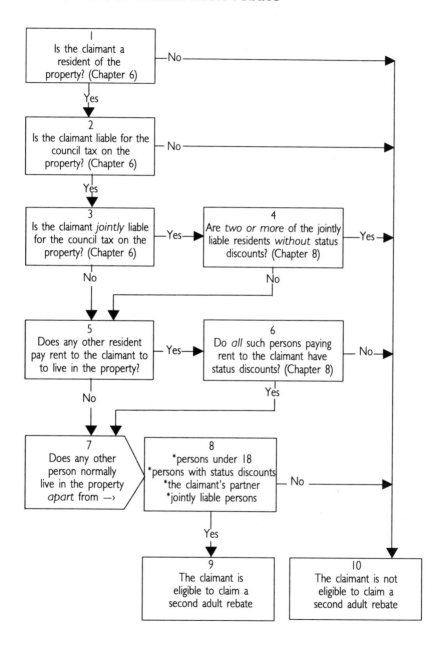

commercial basis. But it does not include a person who:

- is aged under 18 (such people do not count as 'residents' and do not affect the size of the council tax bill);
- is disregarded for the purpose of a council tax discount (such people do not affect the size of the liable person's council tax bill);
- is the claimant's partner who is jointly and severally liable to pay the tax on the dwelling (such people are included in any claim for CTB); *or*
- is a joint owner or tenant with the claimant who is jointly liable to pay the tax on the dwelling (such people can claim CTB for their share of the council tax bill).

Examples

The owner occupier lives with her elderly widowed mother. The owner as the liable person can claim second adult rebate and the mother would be a second adult.

A tenant of a three-bedroomed house lives with her partner who is a full-time student and disregarded for the purpose of a council tax discount. Their 20-year-old daughter and 25-year-old son live with them. The daughter is unemployed and in receipt of income support. The son is in low-paid employment. Either partner may claim the second adult rebate and the adult daughter and son are second adults.

A lone parent lives with her two children aged 10 and 14. There would be no entitlement to second adult rebate as there are no second adults in the dwelling.

How is second adult rebate worked out?

The claimant's second adult rebate is worked out on the basis of:

- the pre-discounted council tax for the dwelling; *and*
- the source and gross income(s) of the second adult(s).

Exhibit 10.4 identifies the amount of second adult rebate (as a percentage of pre-discounted council tax liability) awarded in different circumstances.[34]

Exhibit 10.4 Amount of second adult rebate (1993–94)

Circumstances	*Alternative maximum CTB*
Second adult (or all second adults) in receipt of income support	25 per cent of pre-discounted council tax liability
Gross income of second adult(s) (disregarding any income of persons on income support) less than £105 a week	15 per cent of pre-discounted council tax liability
Gross income of second adult(s) (disregarding any income of persons on income support) not less than £105 a week but less than 135 a week	7.5 per cent of pre-discounted council tax liability

Example

The liable person has capital of £100,000 and earns £60,000 a year. The annual council tax on the dwelling is £800. The liable person lives only with his adult son who is unemployed and in receipt of income support. The liable person is able to claim CTB and receives a second adult rebate of 25 per cent of the council tax, ie £200 a year. Note that the liable person would have been entitled to a discount of £200 had the adult son not been living with him.

Additional second adult rebate in exceptional circumstances

The amount of any second adult rebate may be increased to an extent which does not cause it to be greater than 25 per cent of the pre-discounted council tax liability where the authority considers the claimant's circumstances to be exceptional.[35]

What amount of council tax is used to work out second adult rebate?

The council tax liability used to work out the claimant's second adult rebate is the gross council tax liability on the dwelling less:

- any disability reduction (Chapter 7); *and*
- any transitional reduction (Chapter 9).[36]

Any reduction in council tax liability arising from the granting of a discount (Chapter 8) is ignored for the purpose of second adult rebate. In other words where a discount has been granted it must be added back on to the net amount of council tax to arrive at the figure used in the second adult rebate calculation. The discount itself is still granted.

Apportionment of second adult rebate between liable residents

In contrast to main CTB where there is more than one liable resident the second adult rebate is calculated on the pre-discounted council tax figure for the dwelling as a whole. Any benefit arising is then apportioned equally between all the liable residents (except where the claimant is jointly liable with only a partner).[37] However, no resident receives her or his apportioned share of second adult rebate unless a claim for CTB has also been made by that other liable person.

How is income assessed for second adult rebates?

To obtain second adult rebate the claimant must supply details of the gross income of any second adults living in the dwelling. Gross income for second adult rebate purposes includes the second adult's:

- earnings;
- non-earned income;
- actual income from capital (as opposed to a tariff income), eg building society interest payments.[38]

The following sources of income are totally disregarded:

- any income of a second adult on IS;
- any attendance allowance;
- a disability living allowance;
- the income of someone who is disregarded for the purpose of a council tax discount (Chapter 8) except where s/he has a partner who is not discounted.[39]

In the latter case the disregarded person's gross income, less disregarded income, is included with the partner's. Notifications to claimants of the award, or non-award, of second adult rebate entitlement must include a statement as to the amount of any second adult's gross income used to determine the second adult rebate.

What happens if the claimant is entitled to both forms of CTB?

Claimants may only receive main CTB or second adult rebate but not both at the same time. A claimant may be potentially entitled to both main CTB and second adult rebate. Where this is the case the authority must:

- calculate and compare entitlement to both forms of CTB;
- award the form which is of greatest benefit to the claimant; *and*
- notify the claimant of the lesser and greater amount of main CTB and second adult rebate.[40]

Example

Two joint owners live in the property and are jointly responsible for the council tax liability of £700. One is a full-time student for CTB purposes and is therefore excluded from main CTB entitlement.

The other joint owner is in full-time employment and has claimed CTB. His net income after disregards is £71.55. The claimant is aged over 25 and single – his applicable amount is £44.

Living with the joint owners are two females who are non-dependants of both of the liable persons. The non-dependants are aged 25 and 30. One is unemployed and in receipt of unemployment benefit of £44.65. The other is on income support. The non-dependant on income support is disregarded for non-dependant deduction purposes. For the non-dependant on unemployment benefit there is a £1 non-dependant deduction but this is apportioned between the two liable persons.

The council tax on the dwelling is £700. No disability reduction, discount or transitional reduction applies. Though one of the liable persons is disregarded for the purpose of a council tax discount there are still three adults who are counted as residing in the dwelling. Consequently no discount applies.

The eligible claimant's main CTB is worked out as follows:

A. Net annual CT liability = £700
B. Apportioned CT for CTB purposes (50% of £700) = £350
C. Weekly CT liability = (£350/365) × 7 = £6.7123287
D. Apportioned non-dep. deductions (50% of £1) = £0.50p
E. Maximum CTB entitlement £6.7123287 — £0.50 = £6.2123287
F. Applicable amount = £44
G. Net weekly income after disregards = £71.55
H. Weekly income (£71.55) exceeds applicable amount (£44) by £27.55
I. Tapered excess income (£27.55 × 20%) = £5.51

J.   Weekly CTB entitlement (£6.2123287 — £5.51) = £0.7023287
K.   Annual CTB entitlement = £36.621399, ie (£0.7023287÷7) × 365
L.   Annual CT liability £700 — £36.621399 = £663.38

There is only one liable person who is not disregarded for the purpose of a council tax discount. The two non-dependants are second adults for second adult rebate purposes. Consequently the claimant is also entitled to a second adult rebate as follows:

A.   Council tax liability for second adult rebate = £700
B.   Daily council tax liability = £1.9178082, ie £700÷365
C.   The gross weekly income of the second adults disregarding income support is £44.65, therefore the daily second adult rebate is £0.2876712, ie £1.9178082 × 15% (Exhibit 10.2)
D.   The second adult rebate is apportioned between the number of persons jointly liable, ie £0.1438356 ie £0.2876712÷2
E.   Annual second adult rebate = £52.4999994

The claimant is entitled to both main CTB (£36.62) and second adult rebate but the second adult rebate entitlement is the 'better buy' so it is that form of the benefit which is awarded.

The other liable person in this dwelling – the student disregarded for the purpose of a council tax discount – is not eligible for main CTB but is eligible for a second adult rebate. If he claimed he would be entitled to a second adult rebate of the same amount as the other liable person (ie £52.50).

How are claims for CTB made?

Prior to 1 April 1993

The transitional provisions enabled the authority:

- to waive the need for a CTB claim from people entitled to HB or community charge benefit on 31 March 1993;
- to treat claims for HB or community charge benefit made between 31 August 1992 and 31 March 1993 also as claims for CTB;
- to treat community charge benefit claims made prior to 1 April 1993, but not determined by that date, as community charge benefit claims prior to that date and CTB claims after that date.[41]

From 1 April 1993 onwards

The normal process of claiming CTB is exactly the same as existed with community charge benefit and continues with HB. A claim may be made direct to the authority on its claim form or in some other written form that the authority considers acceptable. Alternatively if a claim is also being made for income support from the local social security office the claimant should complete the NHB1(CTB) claim form found in the IS claim form. The Benefits Agency assesses IS entitlement and sends the NHB1 to the authority together with a decision note that advises the authority as to the claimant's IS entitlement.[42]

Backdating the start of claims

A CTB claim made after 1 April 1993 must be treated as made on that date where:

- it is received by the authority's designated office not more than 56 days after 1 April 1993; *and*
- the claimant is liable for council tax from 1 April 1993.[43]

It should also be treated as made on 1 April 1993 if it is made within 56 days from the date the claimant receives the first council tax demand notice if the claimant is liable for council tax from 1 April.[44] This second rule does not apply, however, where the authority's delay in supplying the first council tax demand notice is due to the claimant's own act or omission. It should be emphasised that the claimant does not have to show good cause for not having claimed earlier under either of these rules and the authority is not subject to any subsidy penalty when it backdates the benefit under these provisions.

Example

An authority has ignored the good practice advice given by the DoE to identify and name all jointly liable persons on council tax demand notices.

In April 1993, it sent out a council tax bill to a dwelling occupied by two joint tenants, A and B, only naming tenant A as a liable person. This has led to a build-up of council tax arrears because tenant B failed to realise she was jointly liable and ought to be making a joint contribution.

In December 1993, following an investigation of the case, the authority subsequently issues a 'joint taxpayer's bill' (see p127) which makes it clear that tenant B has been jointly liable for the council tax on the dwelling since 1 April 1993. However, tenant B is on a low income and claims main CTB two weeks later.

As tenant B was liable for the council tax from 1 April 1993 and has claimed CTB within 56 days of receiving her first demand notice (the joint taxpayer's bill) the benefit authority must automatically backdate her claim to 1 April 1993.

In addition to the above the authority should backdate the effective date of claim for HB where the claimant can prove that she or he had 'continuous good cause' for making a late claim throughout that past period.[45] A claim cannot be backdated for more than 52 weeks. Where a claim is backdated, the amount of CTB the claimant receives (if any) depends on her/his circumstances over the period for which backdating is being sought.

When does CTB change or end?

CTB changes if any of the variables that are used in the original calculation change. For example if the claimant is not on income support and her/his capital or income or applicable amount change, the amount of main CTB needs to be recalculated to reflect the change. The claimant has a duty to report any relevant change of circumstance to the authority. CTB may last for a maximum of 60 weeks or 64 in certain instances but ends early if the claimant is no longer in receipt of IS. The authority should send the claimant a new claim form prior to the end of the benefit period.[46]

Overpayments

The authority may recover overpaid CTB (technically referred to as excess benefit) except where it has arisen due to an official error by the authority or the Benefits Agency and the claimant has not materially contributed or caused the overpayment and could not reasonably have been expected to be aware that it was an overpayment at the time of payment or the receipt of any notification relating to the payment.[47] The authority may seek to recover overpaid CTB by any lawful method. Normally it makes a debit to the claimant's council tax account and should advise the liable person of the increased council tax liability. The authority must also issue separate notification on the CTB overpayment itself.[48]

How is an appeal made against a decision on CTB?

The claimant may request, and the authority must supply, a written explanation of any determination it has made on the claim at any time.[49]

Where the claimant disagrees with a determination s/he has six weeks from the date of the relevant notification in which to make a written request for the authority to carry out an internal review of its determination. Any time the authority takes to supply the written statement of reasons during the initial six-week period extends the time the claimant has to request an internal review. The authority may allow an out of time request for an internal review if the claimant has special reasons for the delay.[50]

Appeals on matters to do with CTB may not be made to the valuation tribunal or valuation appeal committee. If the claimant is still not satisfied with the authority's determination following an internal review s/he has four weeks in which to make a written request for a hearing by the authority's review board. The request should set out the grounds on which the review board is sought.[51] An out of time request for a review board hearing may be made if the review board considers that the claimant has special reasons for the delay.[52] The review board is normally expected to hold its hearing within six weeks of receipt of the claimant's request.[53] The constitution of the review board and its procedures are as described in Chapter 9 in relation to appeals on matters to do with transitional reductions. The review board's decision on CTB entitlement is final and must be implemented by the authority unless challenged by way of judicial review.

CHAPTER ELEVEN

Bills and payments

This chapter explains:

- who has to pay the bill;
- how council tax and also in Scotland, the council water charge is billed;
- the information that the bill must contain;
- the different payments arrangements that may be available;
- the authority's power to come to a special payment arrangement with a liable person;
- what happens if there has been an under- or overpayment of council tax; *and*
- how penalties are collected.

Who has to pay the bill?

Chapter 6 identified the people who are liable for the council tax but in most cases no one need actually pay the tax until a bill (called a demand notice in the legislation) has been issued.[1] If the name of a liable person cannot after reasonable inquiry be ascertained the bill may be addressed to 'The Council Tax Payer'.[2] Practice Note No. 5 (para 1.2) advises that the residents in such a dwelling will then need to ascertain who is the person or persons liable to pay or inform the authority if none of them is liable. Paragraph 4.8 of the Practice Note states that authorities should seek to ensure that their computer systems do not issue bills, etc, in the name of taxpayers who have died. These should normally be sent to the executor.

In Scotland no bill need be issued where the only liable person is a housing body (ie a district council, new town development corporation or Scottish Homes) or an owner who has agreed with the authority that no bill need be served.[3]

People who are married or unmarried partners of the liable person or who have the same degree of legal interest in the dwelling are jointly liable for the bill (Chapter 6). In Scotland, but not England and Wales, someone who is jointly liable with the person or persons named on the bill but whose name is not included on the bill is still liable to make any payments required.[4] In England and Wales no payment can be required of someone who is jointly liable if they have not been included in the bill until a 'joint taxpayers' bill' has been issued.[5] Such a bill must be served within six years of the first day of the financial year to which it relates. It is up to the liable persons themselves exactly how they share out responsibility for the bill.

When should bills be issued?

Each financial year the authority should serve a council tax bill on each chargeable dwelling. In England and Wales this should be done as soon as practicable after the authority first sets a council tax for the year.[6] In Scotland an islands council should serve the bill as soon as practicable after it has first set a council tax and a council water charge for the year. A Scottish regional council should serve the bill as soon as practicable after it has set both those amounts and received intimation of the district's council tax for the year.[7]

Separate bills have to be sent for different financial years and for different dwellings even if the same person is liable for both.[8] In England and Wales, however, one council tax bill may also cover the current and preceding financial year if it is in respect of the same dwelling.[9]

Authorities will want to ensure that bills are produced promptly to maximise their cash flows. The authority's billing timetable should be linked to the tax setting timetable.

How is the bill calculated

Liability to council tax is calculated on a daily basis. However, the bill that is issued at the beginning of the financial year is for the full year. The authority is required to use certain assumptions in estimating what it thinks the council tax will be for the whole year.

The authority must estimate the 'chargeable amount' by taking the relevant amount of council tax for that dwelling (depending on its valuation band) and then make the following assumptions:

- the person will be liable for every day;
- the dwelling's valuation band will not change and it will remain a chargeable dwelling throughout the year;
- any reduction under the disability reduction scheme or transitional reduction scheme (in England and Scotland only) has been

properly calculated and applies throughout the year;
- the bill will be either eligible or not eligible for a discount throughout the year;
- any council tax benefit will apply throughout the year;[10]
- liability for the water charge will apply throughout the year in Scotland.[11]

If more than one reduction applies to the council tax for the band, they must be applied in the following order: disability reduction scheme; discount; transitional reduction and council tax benefit. The authority must ensure that where 100 per cent benefit is awarded that this is equal to the taxpayer's liability.

The bill can also take account of any credits from past periods; penalties due or the repayment of any overpayment of council tax benefit.

Special rules apply if a bill is for a period earlier in the financial year but on the day it is issued, the person is no longer liable for council tax at that address. The bill will either:

- require the payment of the amount due up to the last day of liability (calculated as described above but based on the actual not estimated circumstances); *or*
- if the taxpayer is due a credit, the amount payable (if any) after the credit has been offset against the chargeable amount.[12] This could apply, for example, following a delay in calculating council tax benefit.

A bill which is issued after the end of the year to which it relates must require payment of the amount due for the year, calculated as described above but based on the actual circumstances and after taking account of any credits carried over from earlier years.

How are bills served?

For someone to have to pay the tax the bill must have been served on her/him. Bills may be served by post or delivered to the liable person at her/his usual or last known address or to some other person at the chargeable dwelling or by fixing it to some conspicuous part of the dwelling. In the case of a limited company it should be addressed to its registered office and in the case of a partnership to the principal office of the partnership.

Where a bill has been served in the above manner the date of issue is the date the bill was posted or left at the address. In all other cases it is the date of actual service of the notice. The bill should include the date of issue as it determines such matters as when payment may become due.[13] Practice Note No. 5 reminds authorities to ensure that where a bill is sent by post, the first instalment due under it is payable at least 14 days after the day on which it is delivered to the Post Office. The Practice Note suggests that authorities should maintain records of the days on which bills are delivered to the Post Office so that they can present evidence of the day of issue of any particular bill. One defence against enforcement action (Chapter 12) is for the liable person to show that a bill was not delivered. If the bill has not arrived at the appropriate address the authority needs to serve it again if it wishes to start enforcement proceedings.

What information should the bill contain?

The bill must contain certain prescribed information.[14] There are minor variations between England, Wales and Scotland (Exhibits 11.1 and 11.2). It is for authorities to decide the exact wording and how the information appears on the bill. Practice Note No. 5 (para 2.16) points out that council tax bills cannot deal with community charge arrears. In Wales the use of the Welsh language in relation to council tax bills is not dealt with by the regulations. The Welsh Office and Council of Welsh Districts have agreed a code of practice on bilingual bills reproduced in Annex 3 of the Welsh Office's Practice Note A.

Explanatory notes and information to accompany the bill

The bill should be accompanied by a set of explanatory notes which provide information on: valuation and banding, exempt dwellings, disability reductions, discounts, appeals, CTB, and in England and Scotland an explanation of the transitional reduction scheme. The annex of Practice Note No. 5 and Annex 2 of the Welsh Office's Practice Note A provides examples of such explanatory notes. Additionally in England and Wales the bill, if issued prior to the end of the financial year to which it relates, must also be accompanied by certain additional information explaining the authority's income and expenditure.[15]

When is the bill invalid?

A bill is invalid if it does not contain all the required information. Nevertheless if the failure to comply with these requirements arose

---

Exhibit 11.1   Information to be contained in council tax bills: England and Wales

- The name of the person to whom the bill is addressed or if not known the bill may be addressed to the 'Council Tax Payer';
- the day of issue;
- the period covered by the bill;
- the address of the chargeable dwelling;
- the dwelling's valuation band;
- the amount of council tax per chargeable dwelling for the relevant valuation band for each tier of local government (eg district and county council) including where applicable a specified amount to cover parish or community council expenditure;
- how the amount of the council tax payable has been calculated showing separate amounts of any disability reduction, discount, transitional reduction or CTB;
- the reason for any discount, and a statement of the person's duty to inform the authority of anything that affects entitlement to a discount and the fact that if the person fails without reasonable excuse to comply with that duty the authority may impose a financial penalty of £50;
- the amount (if any) to be credited against the amount of council tax which would otherwise be payable for the relevant year;
- the amount of any penalty, or any overpayment of council tax benefit, being recovered under the bill;
- council tax arrears from the preceding year but only to the extent that they have not already been billed for;
- the amount of council tax payable and how it should be paid;
- the address and telephone number to which enquiries may be made.

---

due to a mistake and the amount to be paid is otherwise correct the bill is treated as valid. The authority must issue a correction as soon as practicable after the mistake has been found.[16]

How is an appeal made against the amount of the bill?

A person aggrieved by any calculation made by an authority of an amount which s/he is liable to pay should write to the authority.

Exhibit 11.2   Information to be contained in council tax bills: Scotland

- The name of the person to whom the bill is addressed of if not known the bill may be addressed to the 'Council Tax Payer';
- the address of the dwelling to which the bill relates;
- the dwelling's valuation band and where a disability reduction has been awarded the alternative valuation band;
- where the dwelling is situated within the area of a regional council, the amounts last set or determined as council tax by that council and by the district council within the area of which the dwelling is situated; and as council water charge by that regional council for the relevant year and the relevant valuation band or, where applicable, the alternative valuation band; or where the relevant dwelling is situated within the area of an islands council, the amounts last set or determined as council tax and council water charge by that council;
- the period within the relevant year to which the bill relates;
- the total amounts payable under the notice in respect of council tax; and the council water charge showing itemised separately in each case the amount of any reductions or additions attributable to:
  - a transitional reduction;
  - a discount;
  - CTB;
  - credits in respect of previous overpayments;
  - penalties; *and*
  - any excess CTB being recovered otherwise than by allowing, for the purposes of calculating the total amount payable under the bill a smaller reduction in respect of CTB than would have been applicable but for the previous over-allowance of such benefit;
- the instalments or other payments required to be paid under the bill and the dates on which, and the manner in which, those payments are to be made;
- the name, address and telephone number of the department or unit of the authority to which enquiries may be made together with a note of the hours during which persons may attend at that department or unit with enquiries or during which they may make enquiries by telephone;

continued

> **Exhibit 11.2** *continued*
>
> - a statement of the duty to inform the authority if a discount should not be granted and the fact that if the person fails without reasonable excuse to comply with that duty the authority may impose a financial penalty (if not already notified in some other way);
> - a general explanation of how any disability reduction, transitional reduction or CTB has been determined (if not already notified in some other way).

This refers to both actual and estimated amounts.[17] The letter should say which decision is wrong and why; for example, because a disability reduction or discount has not been awarded.

For the special rules relating to appeals on transitional reduction and CTB see Chapters 9 and 10. On all other matters the authority has two months in which to consider the representations made. If the authority fails to respond in writing within the two-month period or the aggrieved person is still dissatisfied with the response, an appeal can be made to a valuation tribunal in England and Wales and, via the levying authority, to a valuation appeal committee in Scotland. This should normally be done within four months of the date the grievance was first raised with the authority. An appeal cannot, however, be made on the basis that any assumption the authority is required to make about the future may prove to be inaccurate.[18] The council tax bill must still be paid while the appeal is outstanding.

What payment arrangements are possible?

Most taxpayers have a right to pay by instalments. The 'normal' method of payment is by way of ten monthly instalments.[19] The authority may, however, adopt a variety of different payment arrangements, ie:

- in England and Wales the council tenant instalment scheme (in Scotland the authority may establish an agency arrangement with a housing body which then establishes its own payment arrangements[20]);
- special arrangements with the liable person;
- discounted lump sum payments; *and*
- discounts for non-cash payments.

Each of the possible arrangements is considered below.

How many instalments are available?

Where the bill is issued:
- up to 30 April of the relevant year payments under the statutory scheme are to be made in ten monthly instalments;
- from 1 May onwards the monthly instalments must equal one less than the number of whole months remaining in the financial year;
- between 1 January and 31 March in the relevant year the total amount due is payable in a single instalment on the day specified on the bill.[21]

The instalments must be payable one month after another but the authority may choose which month to start with and state this on the bill.[22]

Amount of the instalment

The amount of the instalment is worked out by dividing the total amount of the bill by the number of instalments. If this gives an amount which is a multiple of a pound, the instalments shall be of that amount.[23]

Example

The council tax is £500 and payments are to be by way of ten instalments. The amount of each instalment will be £50.

Where the total amount due divided by the number of instalments does not give an amount which is a multiple of a pound the amount payable should be divided by the number of instalments and rounded to the nearest pound. Amounts ending in 50p should be rounded up. This amount is the amount of the instalments other than the first. This amount should be multiplied by the number of instalments less one and the resulting amount should be subtracted from the total amount payable. The amount remaining is the amount of the first instalment.[24]

Example

The council tax is £500 and payments are to be by way of nine instalments
The amount of all but the first instalment will be £56
(ie £500 ÷ 9 = £55.5555)
The first instalment should be £52
(ie £500 — (£56 × 8 instalments))

If someone has only a small amount to pay by way of the council tax the instalment method would be a very expensive way for the authority to collect it. Consequently the legislation gives authorities the power not to accept any instalment where the payment would be less than £5. Where the total amount payable is less than £10 the authority may request payment of that amount in a single instalment. Where the total amount payable is £10 or more the authority may reduce the number of instalments to the greatest number that allows individual instalments of at least £5.[25]

What arrangements can the authority make for council tenants?

In Scotland the authority may establish an agency arrangement with a housing body, ie the district council, Scottish Homes or a new town development corporation. It is then for that housing body to establish appropriate payment arrangements.[26]

In England and Wales an authority may resolve to set up an instalment scheme for its council tenants so that they may pay their council tax on the same day they pay their rent. This means that if council tenants pay their rent weekly, for example, the authority may also allow them to pay their council tax weekly.[27] The scheme may also be drawn up so that it continues to apply during any period in the year when rent is not payable so long as such a period follows a period in which rent was payable. To date only a minority of authorities have established such schemes.

To meet the requirements of the legislation the scheme must:

- apply to all council tenants;
- have effect for all financial years unless varied or revoked;
- only be varied in its operation if this is agreed prior to the authority first setting its council tax for the relevant year;
- not be revoked later than 31 December of the year immediately preceding the beginning of the financial year in which it will no longer apply;
- not have fewer than ten instalments and no more than 52;
- require the first instalment to be payable no earlier than 14 days after the day on which the bill was issued;
- require instalments to be payable on such day in each interval as is specified in the scheme;
- require the last instalment to be paid before the end of the relevant year; *and*
- provide for the determination of the amount of any instalment

where the aggregate amount divided by the number of instalments does not give an amount which is a multiple of 10 pence.[28]

What happens to instalments when liability ends?

No payments of instalments under either the statutory schemes or in England and Wales the council tenant's scheme are due once a person is no longer liable for the tax and in Scotland the water charge. Where more than one person is jointly liable whether named on the original bill or not this only applies where none of them are liable. In England and Wales if the only person or persons who are liable are people who were not named on the original bill then the authority must issue a joint taxpayers' notice on them.[29]

Where the originally liable person or persons are no longer liable the authority must serve a notice on the formerly liable person or where there was joint liability at least one of the jointly liable persons. The notice should state the actual amount due up to the day liability ended. This should be done as soon as practicable after the ending of liability.[30]

If the amount due is less than the combined amounts of any instalments which should have been paid the difference is first used to meet any arrears on those past instalments. The liable person may require the authority to repay any residual overpayment. Where no such request has been made the authority may decide either to repay it or to credit it against the liable person's liability.[31] It cannot be used to meet any other debt such as arrears of community charge.

If the amount due is greater than the combined amount of the past instalments the liable person should pay the outstanding amount to the authority. The authority must allow at least 14 days from the issuing of the bill for this amount to be paid.[32]

If the formerly liable person becomes liable for the tax once again in the authority in the same financial year the matter is dealt with afresh. Any previous overpayment of tax by the liable person may however be credited against the subsequent liability.

What happens to instalments when liability changes?

The instalment schemes are based on the assumption that the liable person's or persons' circumstances will remain the same throughout the year. Liability may change, however, because:

- the council tax changes as a result of budgets being capped by central government;
- the dwelling becomes exempt;
- the dwelling's valuation band changes;
- discount entitlement changes;
- entitlement to a disability reduction or in England or Scotland transitional reduction changes;
- entitlement to CTB changes; *or*
- liability to pay the water charge in Scotland changes.[33]

Following each of these circumstances the authority must adjust the remaining instalments (if any), as soon as practicable after the change, so that they accord with the new amounts due.[34] As many adjustments may be made as the circumstances require. The authority must also serve a revised bill (an adjustment notice) on a liable person each time an adjustment is made. This should state:

- the revised estimated liability for the relevant year assuming no further changes; *and*
- the amount of any instalments that remain 14 or more days after the issue of the notice.

In England and Wales where instalments are payable under the statutory scheme, and additional amounts are now due as a result of the change, the payments must be fixed in accordance with the rules for that scheme (see above). In Scotland the authority has the discretion to set the amount of each remaining instalment. Where no further instalments are due the additional amount must be paid as a lump sum within a period set by the authority. The authority must give the liable person at least 14 days from the date of issue of the bill to pay the amount owing.

Where the revised amount is less than the combined amounts of the instalments payable before the change, the liable person can require the authority to repay the overpayment to the extent that it exceeds any liability. If the liable person has not made such a request the authority may decide either to repay it or credit it against that person's subsequent liability.[35]

What special payment arrangements may be agreed?

An authority and a liable person may agree that the council tax be paid in such manner as they arrange between them.[36] These special payment arrangements may be entered into either before or after a bill has been issued, though in England and Wales if there is joint liability the arrangement can only be entered with someone named on the bill. Special payment arrangements may prove useful where the liable person is facing financial problems.

These special agreements may make provision for the ending or adjustment of payments. They may also allow for the making of fresh estimates if the original estimate turns out to be wrong. If the special arrangement is entered into after the bill has been issued, it may make provision dealing with the treatment of any sums paid in accordance with the statutory instalment scheme or, additionally in England and Wales, the council tenant instalment scheme.

A bill issued under such a special arrangement shall (as the billing authority determines) require payment of the amount concerned:

- within a set period of not less than 14 days after the day the bill is issued; *or*
- by instalments of such amounts as are specified on the bill and payable at such intervals and on such day in each interval as is specified.

Special agreements do not attract the normal enforcement procedures (Chapter 12). While the agreement may be oral Practice Note No. 5 (para 3.14) advises authorities to ensure that the agreement is in writing and sets out the procedures to be followed in the event of non-payment.

When can the authority offer a discount for lump sum payments?

The authority may decide to encourage payment of the council tax by way of a lump sum as this improves its cash flow and reduces its collection costs. The benefits and costs of such an arrangement, not only to the authority but to all taxpayers, need to be considered carefully. To encourage this method of lump sum payments the authority can offer a discount.[37]

If the authority is to operate such discount arrangements it must:

- resolve to operate such a scheme and the amount to be discounted on or before the day it first sets its council tax for the year; *and*
- apply the scheme in the same way to people who pay the same number of instalments in the year.

Furthermore for a lump sum to qualify for a discount:

- at least two instalments of council tax must be payable; *and*
- the single lump sum payment must be made on or before the day on which the first instalment is due.

When can the authority offer a discount for non-cash payments?

Various methods are available to pay the council tax but some are more cost-effective for authorities than others. From the authority's point of view direct debit has the most advantages and direct debit mandate forms are often sent out with demand notices to encourage the use of this payment method. In addition the authority is able to offer a discount to taxpayers if they use such non-cash methods of payment.[38]

Again the authority should consider the costs and benefits of such arrangements. The size of the discount and the cases where non-cash payments are to be accepted must be decided by the authority on or before the day it first sets the council tax for the year. Such a determination may be revoked at any time and if revoked on or before the day the authority first sets its council tax for the relevant year, it may be replaced by a fresh determination.

Where an adjustment must be made to the amount paid and the amount has been paid by a discounted non-cash payment the instalment or other payment by reference to which the discounted amount was accepted must be treated as having been paid in full. Any sum to be repaid, or credited against any subsequent liability, however, is reduced by the same proportion as was allowed for the discount.

What happens if an estimate has been based on an incorrect assumption?

Where payments are made under the statutory instalment scheme or, in England and Wales, the council tenants' instalments scheme incorrect assumptions are dealt with as described above. In other circumstances, for example where a lump sum payment has been made it may become clear during the course of the year that an estimated amount has been based on an incorrect assumption. For example the position regarding entitlement to a discount may change part way through the year. In such circumstances the authority may, or if required by the liable person must, make a calculation of the appropriate amount that currently appears due for the year.[39]

Having made such a calculation if:

- the new amount is greater than the estimated amount the authority should bill the liable person and require the interim payment within a period of not less than 14 days from the date of issue of the bill;
- the new amount is less than the estimated amount the authority should notify the liable person accordingly and make an interim repayment.

In England and Wales the one exception to the rule requiring repayment arises where the overpayment of council tax has arisen because the liable person is no longer liable to make payments on one dwelling but becomes immediately liable to make payments to the same authority on another dwelling. In these circumstances the authority may credit the overpayment against the new liability. This exception does not apply in relation to overpayments of lump sum payments.[40]

What happens if there has been an under- or overpayment?

The actual amount owed to the authority will be known for certain only at the end of the financial year or when the taxpayer's liability ends. Consequently another bill is required where a previous bill has been issued by the authority for a financial year, or part of a financial year, and the payment or payments required to be made were in fact more than, or less than, the actual liability; and there has been no appropriate adjustment (see above). The authority should, as soon as practicable after the end of the year or the part of a year, serve a new notice on the liable person. This should state the actual amount due and adjust the amounts required to be paid under the previous bill.[41]

If the amount stated in the new notice is greater than the amount previously required the liable person must pay the difference within a period specified by the authority. This period must be at least 14 days following the issue of the new bill.[42]

If there has been an overpayment of council tax and if the liable person requires a refund this must be given. In any other case the authority may decide either to repay the amount in question to the liable person or credit it against any future council tax liability.[43]

Again the exception to this rule requiring repayment is where the overpayment of council tax has arisen because the liable person is no longer liable to make payments on one dwelling but is immediately liable to make payments to the same authority on another dwelling. In these particular circumstances the authority may require the amount of any overpayment, instead of being repaid, to be credited against the new liability.[44] This exception does not apply in the case of lump sum payments.

What if there has been an overpayment and the authority refuses to repay it?

In England and Wales the regulations make explicit the fact that any sum identified in this chapter which the authority is required to repay to the liable person but which the authority is reluctant to repay may be recovered via civil debt procedure through the county court.[45]

How are penalty payments collected?

In certain circumstances a penalty may be imposed by the authority on a person:

- who fails to respond to a request for information for the purpose of identifying the liable person (Chapter 6);
- who fails to notify the authority that the dwelling is no longer exempt (Chapter 5); or
- who fails to notify the authority that they are no longer liable for the same level of discount (Chapter 8).

Such a penalty may be collected by the authority by:

- including it on the council tax bill (see above); or
- sending a separate bill for the penalty.[46]

In the latter case the authority must give not less than 14 days for the bill to be paid. Where the imposition of a penalty is subject to an appeal or in England and Wales arbitration:

- no bill can be issued for the recovery of a penalty;
- no amount is payable in respect of the penalty.[47]

If the penalty is subject to such an appeal or, additionally in England and Wales, arbitration after the issue of a bill, the proportions of the instalments on the bill attributable to the penalty are not payable until the appeal or arbitration is finally disposed of, abandoned or fails for non-prosecution.[48]

Where an amount has been paid in respect of a penalty which is later quashed either by the authority or following an order of a valuation tribunal, valuation appeal committee, the High Court or Court of Session, the authority which imposed the penalty must repay it. This can be done by deducting an amount from any other penalty, council tax and in Scotland council water charge that is owed to the authority and repaying any balance.[49]

CHAPTER TWELVE

Enforcement

This chapter explains:

- the statutory enforcement process in England and Wales;
- what happens if instalments are not paid;
- what a liability order is and its implications;
- the available recovery methods; *and*
- the statutory enforcement process in Scotland.

This chapter describes the statutory enforcement process, ie the way in which the authority can recover unpaid amounts. The process in Scotland is distinctly different from that which operates in England and Wales. The English and Welsh process is described first and then the Scottish one. Some elements, however, such as the ability to make deductions from income support, are common to both systems.

The authority is free to agree a special payment arrangement with a taxpayer (Chapter 11). The re-scheduling of payments under such an arrangement may often be the most appropriate response when the taxpayer is in arrears. In England and Wales once a special arrangement has been entered into the statutory enforcement provisions described in this chapter do not apply automatically. Practice Note No. 9 recommends that any agreement between the English or Welsh authority and the taxpayer should include the enforcement procedures that will apply in the case of non-payment. In many cases these may be exactly the same as the statutory enforcement procedures.

At any point in the enforcement process recovery action must stop if the outstanding amount (including costs) is paid.

What is the statutory enforcement process in England and Wales?

Exhibit 12.1 provides an overview of the statutory enforcement process in England and Wales.

Exhibit 12.1 The statutory enforcement process in England and Wales

(Action stops if the amount due is paid)

```
┌─────────────────┐   ┌─────────────┐   ┌─────────────────┐   ┌─────────────┐
│        1        │   │      2      │   │        3        │   │      4      │
│      BILL       │→  │ INSTALMENT  │→  │ REMINDER (OR    │→  │ FULL YEAR'S │
│ (Demand notice  │   │   MISSED    │   │ FINAL) NOTICE   │   │  TAX DUE    │
│ issued at least │   │             │   │ (Seven days     │   │             │
│ 14 days before  │   │             │   │ given to pay    │   │             │
│ 1st instalment  │   │             │   │ missed          │   │             │
│ is due)         │   │             │   │ instalment)     │   │             │
└─────────────────┘   └─────────────┘   └─────────────────┘   └─────────────┘

┌─────────────────┐   ┌─────────────┐   ┌─────────────┐   ┌─────────────┐
│        5        │   │      6      │   │      7      │   │      8      │
│ COMPLAINT TO    │→  │   SUMMONS   │→  │  LIABILITY  │→  │ OBTAINING OF│
│ MAGISTRATES     │   │             │   │   ORDER     │   │ INFORMATION │
└─────────────────┘   └─────────────┘   └─────────────┘   └─────────────┘

┌───────────┐ ┌───────────┐ ┌───────────┐ ┌───────────┐ ┌───────────┐ ┌───────────┐
│     9     │ │    10     │ │    11     │ │    12     │ │    13     │ │    14     │
│ATTACHMENT │ │ATTACHMENT │ │ DEDUCTION │ │ CHARGING  │ │INSOLVENCY │ │ DISTRESS  │
│OF EARNINGS│ │    OF     │ │   FROM    │ │  ORDER    │ │           │ │           │
│           │ │ALLOWANCES │ │  INCOME   │ │           │ │           │ │           │
│           │ │           │ │ SUPPORT   │ │           │ │           │ │           │
└───────────┘ └───────────┘ └───────────┘ └───────────┘ └───────────┘ └───────────┘

┌─────────────────┐   ┌─────────────┐   ┌─────────────┐
│       15        │   │     16      │   │     17      │
│ APPLICATION     │→  │   MEANS     │→  │   PRISON    │
│ FOR A           │   │  ENQUIRY    │   │  AND/OR     │
│ WARRANT OF      │   │             │   │ REMISSION   │
│ COMMITMENT      │   │             │   │             │
└─────────────────┘   └─────────────┘   └─────────────┘
```

What happens if an instalment is not paid?

If the bill has been correctly issued but the taxpayer fails to pay an instalment under the statutory instalment scheme or the council tenant instalment scheme (Chapter 11) the authority must issue a reminder.[1] The reminder requires payment to be made within seven days.[2] It must include:

- a note of the instalment, or instalments, that have not been paid;
- a statement informing the taxpayer that if no, or insufficient, payment is made to cover any instalments that are, or will become, due within seven days of the issue of the reminder the right to pay by instalments is lost and the full year's tax becomes payable after a further seven days.

This reminder also acts as a notice of impending enforcement action. If a reminder is issued and there is a failure to pay within seven days then a 'final notice' is not required before the authority applies for a liability order.

If two reminders are issued during the financial year the taxpayer becomes liable for the whole of the outstanding amount following a third failure to pay. No further reminder is required.[3] The taxpayer should be informed of the consequences of a third failure to pay on the second reminder notice.[4]

A final notice is required if a third failure to pay occurs. It should state every amount that the authority would seek on a liability order, unless that amount is the same as that on the second reminder.[5] When someone defaults from a special payment arrangement a final notice should also be issued. In the case of joint taxpayers a final notice may be addressed to all of them.[6] In all cases once the outstanding amount has become payable following a reminder or after seven days following the issuing of a final notice the authority may seek a liability order from the magistrates' courts.[7]

Joint liability

If a bill has been issued in joint names the authority can seek to recover the unpaid amount from anyone who is jointly liable. If a joint bill has not been issued then to invoke joint liability the authority must send a notice to those who are jointly liable but who have not previously been issued with a bill before any recovery action can be taken against them. The jointly liable person must be given at least 14 days in which to pay the bill. If payment is not received a reminder must be served on the jointly liable person. If payment is not received after seven days an application may be made to a magistrates' court for a liability order.

Write-offs

While authorities normally pursue debts until they are recovered, in certain instances it may be appropriate for an authority to consider writing off debts which are not cost-effective to pursue or in cases of particular financial hardship.

What is a liability order and what are its implications?

The liability order provides the authority with a variety of recovery options (see below). Such an order cannot be obtained if the authority has not issued a reminder or final notice as described above. Before seeking a liability order the authority should, as a matter of good practice, carry out checks to see whether the debtor:

- is entitled to council tax benefit (Chapter 10);
- has made a claim for benefit that has yet to be processed; or
- has made an appeal (Chapter 13).

Where any of these circumstances apply the authority may suspend recovery action until the benefit entitlement has been sorted out or the appeal decided. Legally, however, a person is liable for the full amount of the council tax demanded by the authority and a magistrates' court can order payment. In *R v Bristol Magistrates' Court, ex parte Willsman and another*,[7a] for example, it was decided, in relation to the community charge, that the magistrates' court could order payment despite the fact that a claim for community charge benefit had been made and despite the fact that the authority had failed to determine the claim within the statutory period.

The one exception to this general rule requiring payment is that no amount is payable in respect of a penalty if there is an outstanding appeal against its imposition (Chapter 13). It should be emphasised, however, that the decision to seek a liability order is a discretionary one.[8] Consequently the authority must consider the relevant facts of the individual case and not act in an unreasonable manner.[9] In the *Bristol case* (see above) the applicants contended that the authority's decision to lay complaints against them in the magistrates' court constituted an unreasonable exercise of the discretion given by the regulation (and also given by the equivalent council tax regulation).[10]

The evidence showed, however, that it was, in fact, the authority's practice not to apply for liability orders in cases where it knew that benefit applications were pending. In this case the relevant liability orders had been sought in error. Where an authority does seek liability orders knowing that benefit claims are pending it is possible to argue on judicial review that this practice constitutes an unreasonable exercise of the authority's discretionary power.

Obtaining a liability order

To obtain a liability order the authority applies to the magistrates' court for a summons.[11] To do this the authority lays a complaint before a justice of the peace, or the justices' clerk,[12] identifying the debtor against whom it wishes a summons to be issued. This must be done within six years of the day on which the amount became due.[13] It is usually a collective action for all debtors at specific times of the year. A single summons is only able to cover one person. Practice Note No. 9 advises authorities that if a single reminder is issued to two or more persons the authorities' systems must be able to produce separate summonses for each of the individuals named on the reminder.

The summons directs the debtor to attend the court to show good reason why a liability order should not be made. No warrant may be issued for the arrest of someone who does not appear and in reality many people who have been summoned do not attend. The 'hearing' takes place in their absence. The summons is not a prescribed form but should set out the amount outstanding. It may also include the costs reasonably incurred. These include not only the court's administration costs but also the costs associated with the authority's action. While it is likely that authorities will have discussed a scale of fees with the clerk to the justices, Practice Note No. 9 points out that the court may wish to be satisfied that the amount claimed by way of costs is no more than that reasonably incurred by the authority.

Service of summons

A summons may be served on someone by:

- posting it to that person's usual or last known place of abode;
- delivering it to the person;
- leaving it at her or his usual or last known address;
- in the case of a company leaving it, or sending it by post to its registered office; *or*
- by leaving it at, or sending it by post to, an address given by the person as an address at which service will be accepted.[14]

Payment of the outstanding amount

If the outstanding amount plus costs are paid then the authority cannot continue with the application for a liability order.[15] If the amount outstanding has been paid but not the costs then a liability order can still be made for the costs alone.[16]

The hearing

Where summonses have been issued, and payments not made, magistrates hear the authority's applications for liability orders. Normally a number are heard on the same day.

Representatives

The officer representing the authority must be duly authorised under s223 of the Local Government Act 1972. A copy of the resolution authorising the officer certified by the proper officer of the authority should be available when the officer is conducting proceedings on behalf of the authority.

The person summoned may represent her/his own case without a legal representative. In addition, the case of *R v Leicester City Justices, ex parte Barrow and another*,[16a] confirmed that the person summoned also has a right to the assistance of a friend who is not a lawyer. Such a friend can sit beside the defendant in court and assist by taking notes, prompting and quietly giving advice on the conduct of the case. Such an adviser has commonly become known as a 'McKenzie friend'. It is sensible to mention to the justices or their clerk that such an adviser is present. The court may however exclude such a 'friend' from giving assistance if there is good reason to believe that s/he is interfering with the proper administration of justice. The justices' clerk is also able to provide assistance if this can be done without prejudicing her/his impartiality. The defendant is also entitled to bring books, papers, pens, pencils, spectacles, a hearing aid and any other material thought appropriate.[17]

Grounds for a liability order

An order must be made if the magistrates are satisfied that:

- the sum is payable by the person concerned; *and*
- has not been paid.[18]

Practice Note No. 9 summarises the matters on which the authority must satisfy the court if an order is to be made, ie:

- the council tax has been fixed by resolution of the authority;
- the sums have been demanded in accordance with the regulations;
- full payment of amounts due has not been made by the due date;
- a reminder, second reminder or a final notice has been issued as required;
- the sum has not been paid within seven days of the reminder or final notice being issued and the full amount has become payable;
- the summons has been served for the amount outstanding at least seven days after the sum became payable; *and*
- the full sum claimed has not been paid.

The defences available to the taxpayer are:

- the amount has not been demanded in accordance with the regulations; *or*
- the amount has been paid; *or*
- that s/he is not the person named on the summons.

Any matter relating to liability which could be the subject of an appeal to a valuation tribunal (Chapter 13) may not be raised in liability order proceedings.[19] This includes matters such as:

- whether or not the debtor is a liable person;
- whether or not the dwelling is a chargeable dwelling;
- entitlement to a disability reduction; *or*
- entitlement to a discount.

Evidence

In the course of community charge recovery action computer evidence was held to be inadmissible on the grounds that it was hearsay. The council tax enforcement regulations make clear that the authority may offer in evidence any statement contained in a document, including a statement which has been computer generated, which it believes would further its case at the hearing so long as:

- the document constitutes or forms part of a record compiled by the authority;
- direct oral evidence of any fact stated would have been admissible; *and*
- where the document has been produced by a computer, it must be accompanied by a certificate which:
  - identifies the document and the computer by which it was produced,
  - includes a statement that at all material times the computer

was operating properly, or if not, that defect did not affect the production of the document or its accuracy, *and*

- is signed by a person occupying a responsible position in relation to the operation of the computer.

The order

The court may make a liability order for one person or may make several liability orders in the form of a schedule. The different forms are prescribed in the regulations.[20] In either case the form identifies the aggregate amount that can be recovered using the methods identified below. If the full sum claimed has been reduced, for example as the result of the award of council tax benefit, the liability order will be for a greater sum than the amount payable. In such cases the order remains in force and the excess amount is treated as paid. If following the issue of an order the debtor is found to owe more than the amount specified the authority can only enforce up to the limit stated in the order. It must seek a new order to enforce the outstanding balance.

What are the available recovery methods?

The liability order provides the authority with the power to:

- obtain information about the financial circumstances of the debtor (and thus assess the best course of recovery action);
- make an attachment of earnings order (AEO);
- make an attachment order on an elected member's allowances;
- apply to the Benefits Agency for deductions to be made from the debtor's IS;
- use bailiffs or in-house staff to levy distress;
- apply for a charging order against the dwelling in respect of which the debtor's liability arose; *and*
- apply to bankrupt the debtor (if s/he is an individual) or to wind up the company (where the debtor is a corporate body).

Information the debtor must provide

Once the liability order has been made, and for as long as the amount in question remains unpaid,[21] the authority may request the debtor to provide the following information:

- the name and address of an employer;
- the debtor's earnings or expected earnings;
- information on statutory deductions from pay (which must be

disregarded in calculating the amount to be deducted under an
AEO);

- the debtor's work or identity number or other such identifier used
  by her/his employer;
- information on existing attachment of earnings orders;
- information on other sources of income, eg benefit, councillors'
  allowances; *and*
- whether there is anyone jointly liable with the debtor for the whole
  or any part of the amount for which the order was made.[22]

The debtor does not have to supply the information if the request is
not made in writing; or if the information is not in her/his possession
or control.[23] Otherwise the debtor must provide the information
within 14 days of the request being made.[24] The debtor does not,
however, have to advise the authority of a change of circumstance
unless the authority makes a fresh request for the relevant
information. Where a liability order has been granted for those
who are jointly liable the authority can require this information from
any or all of them. If the debtor fails, without reasonable excuse, to
supply the requested information s/he is guilty of a criminal offence
and may be fined by the magistrates' court up to a current maximum
of level 2.[25] If the debtor knowingly or recklessly supplies
information which is false in a material particular, s/he is also
guilty of a criminal offence and may be fined up to a maximum of
level 3.[26]

Relationship between recovery methods

The authority may decide which recovery method it wishes to use in
each case and may use it more than once but it may not pursue more
than one method at any one time[27] and in the case of joint liability
only against one person at a time.[28]

Example

An AEO has been made, the authority cannot use bailiffs to distrain the
debtor's goods until it formally ends the AEO. The debtor is made
unemployed and claims income support. If the authority cancels the AEO it
can seek deductions from the claimant's income support. The debtor regains
employment. The authority may once again make an AEO.

What is distress?

This remedy enables the authority to seize the debtor's possessions, a process known as levying distress. The possessions may be seized from anywhere in England or Wales and sold, usually by auction, to pay off:

- the outstanding sum forming part of the amount in respect of which the liability order was issued; *and*
- the charges associated with the levying of distress.[29]

Distraint can be prevented if all amounts due have been paid.[30] Once distraint has been levied, a sale can be prevented by full payment of the sums due prior to sale.[31] Practice Note No. 9 advises that, while distress can be an effective recovery method, authorities should consider other methods (such as attachment of earnings or deductions from income support) in preference to distress as an initial enforcement option. If some other method of recovery is actually in force the authority has no power to levy distress.[32]

Goods that cannot be distrained

The authority cannot seize certain goods[33] including:

- goods on lease or hire purchase; *and*
- goods used by the debtor but belonging to the landlord or other members of the household.

The authority's power to levy distress does not override enactments which protect certain goods from distress.[34] Additionally the council tax regulations specifically protect the following items from seizure:

- the debtor's tools, books, vehicles and other items of equipment necessary to the debtor for her/his personal use in employment, business or vocation; *and*
- clothing, bedding, furniture, household equipment and provisions necessary for the basic needs of the debtor and family.[35]

General powers of bailiffs

Distress can be carried out by anyone with the written authorisation of the authority. In practice most authorities use private firms of bailiffs to collect unpaid council tax. The written authorisation must be shown on request.[36] The legal position regarding bailiffs is uncertain but the existing case law suggests that bailiffs have the following powers. Where a building contains goods which a bailiff is entitled to seize the bailiff has a right to enter that building peacefully. The bailiff may enter a property peacefully through an unlocked door or through an open window. S/he may not force a locked door or open a closed window (even if it is not locked). Bailiffs cannot obtain a court order to gain entry to any property nor can the occupier be sent to prison for merely refusing to allow bailiffs to enter.

Having gained peaceful entry to the building, the bailiff is then entitled to enter and search any room for the debtor's goods and seize them without being held liable as a trespasser. S/he is entitled to force any inner door which is locked. This applies even to those rooms which the debtor does not occupy. It also applies to any building where the defaulter's goods are located and not just the one s/he occupies as a main residence. Once the bailiff has gained peaceful entry, with or without the consent of the occupier, withdrawing that consent or refusing permission to enter other parts of the property are of no effect. This applies even where the occupier was misled into believing that the bailiff only wanted to discuss the situation and not levy distress on that occasion.

There are a number of different forms of possession in relation to distress,[37] ie:

- walking possession – where the debtor signs an agreement which enables the goods to stay on the premises without physical supervision by the bailiff until payment is made or the goods are eventually removed for sale;
- close possession is the same except that the bailiff stays on the premises for at least the greater part of the day in physical possession of the goods;
- removal – where the bailiff takes goods away with a view to selling them.

The most common form of possession in a council tax arrears case is walking possession. Having taken walking possession of the debtor's goods the bailiff cannot be refused entry if s/he has to return to remove those goods at a later date. The bailiff would be entitled to force entry under these circumstances.

Many bailiffs, unable to gain entry to a community charge debtor's home, attempted to carry out what was referred to as 'constructive distress'. This involved posting a 'notice of distress' through the letterbox claiming that (usually unspecified) goods on the premises have been seized. In *Evans v South Ribble District Council*,[37a] it was held that it is not possible to carry out constructive distress in this way. For a seizure of goods to be lawful the bailiff must enter the property, except in the exceptional circumstances where the goods s/he is attempting to seize are on the point of removal and those doing the removing are directly confronted.

The person carrying out the distress must leave:

- a copy of Regulation 45 and of Schedule 5 (charges connected with distress) to the Council Tax (Administration and Enforcement) Regulations 1992 (as amended);
- a memorandum setting out the appropriate amount.

Additionally a copy of any close or walking possession agreement entered into must be handed to the debtor.[38]

Charges connected with distress

The charges connected with distress are detailed in Exhibit 12.2.

Practice Note No. 9 advises that authorities should ensure that they are not adding unduly to any financial hardship the debtor might be facing. Authorities should, for instance, agree with their bailiffs how long agreements should last. In the case of any dispute as to the charges connected with the distress the debtor, or the authority, may apply to the district judge of the county court for the amount of the charge to be set by the judge.[39]

Code of practice

The authority is responsible for ensuring that the activities of its bailiffs comply with the law. Practice Note No. 9 advises that authorities may like to ensure the status of its bailiffs by requiring that they have a certificate from a county court in relation to distress for rent. While no such certificate is formally required to levy distress for the council tax the process of registering for a certificate does require two referees and a bond to be provided as security for proper conduct.

The Practice Note also suggests that the authority should issue guidelines on the procedures to be adopted by bailiffs and provides some good practice suggestions. The Public Law Project has issued a Code of Practice on Local Authorities' Use of Bailiffs in the Enforcement of Community Charge and Council Tax. This may be used as a model by authorities.[40] Where an authority has adopted such a Code of Practice advisers may find it useful to obtain a copy and use it in discussions with the authority.

Sale of goods

Practice Note No. 9 advises that authorities should ensure that they

Exhibit 12.2   Charges connected with distress

Matter connected with distress   *Charge*

A. For making a visit to premises with a view to levying distress (where no levy is made):

- where the visit is the first or only such visit;   £15
- where the visit is the second such visit.   £12.50

B. For levying distress: The lesser of:

- the amount of the costs and fees reasonably incurred; *and*
- where the sum due at the time of the levy does not exceed £100, £15; *or*
- where the sum due at the time of the levy exceeds £100, 15 per cent on the first £100 of the sum due, 4 per cent on the next £400, 2.5 per cent on the next £1,500, 1 per cent on the next £8,000 and 0.25 per cent on any additional sum.

(The sum due at any time for these purposes means so much of the amount in respect of which the liability order concerned was made as is outstanding at the time.)

C. For one attendance with a vehicle with a view to the removal of goods (where, following the levy, goods are not removed):   Reasonable costs and fees incurred.

continued

Exhibit 12.2 *continued*

Matter connected with distress	*Charge*
D. For the removal and storage of goods for the purposes of sale:	Reasonable costs and fees incurred.
E. For the possession of goods	
• for close possession (the person in possession to provide her/his own board):	£10 a day
• for walking possession:	10 pence a day
F. For appraisement of an item distrained, at the request in writing of the debtor:	Reasonable fees and expenses of the broker appraising.
G. For other expenses of, and commission on, a sale by auction:	
• where the sale is held on the auctioneer's premises:	The auctioneer's commission fee and out-of-pocket expenses (but not exceeding in aggregate 15 per cent of the sum realised), together with reasonable costs and fees incurred in respect of advertising.
• where the sale is held on the debtor's premises:	The auctioneer's commission fee (but not exceeding 7.5 per cent of the sum realised), together with the auctioneer's out-of-pocket expenses and reasonable costs and fees incurred in respect of advertising.
H. Where no sale takes place by reason of payment	Reasonable costs and fees incurred in respect of advertising.

obtain the best price for the goods. Goods are usually sold by auction. The sale should not normally take place until at least five days after the removal of goods. The debtor or an adviser should try and prevent the sale of goods wherever possible since it is not a cost-effective way of clearing the debt from the debtor's point of view. The proceeds from the sale usually only represent a fraction of the goods' replacement value. If a sale does take place, the balance of moneys, minus the costs associated with the sale, should be returned to the debtor.

Appeals against distress

A person who is aggrieved by the levy of, or attempt to levy, a distress has the right of appeal to a magistrates' court.[41] A justice of the peace (or a justices' clerk)[42] should be requested to issue a summons requiring the relevant authority to appear before the court and answer the complaint.[43] A distress is not considered unlawful, however, simply because of a defect in the liability order.[44]

If the court is satisfied that a levy was irregular it may:

- order any goods taken to be returned if they are still in the authority's possession; *and*
- award an amount of money for any goods distrained and sold.

The award is equal to the amount which, in the opinion of the court, would be awarded by way of special damages in respect of the goods if proceedings were brought in trespass or otherwise in connection with the irregularity.[45] If the court is satisfied that the levy was irregular it may also make an order requiring the authority to desist from levying in such a manner.[46]

What is an attachment of earnings?

An authority which has obtained a liability order against a person who is employed may arrange, in appropriate circumstances, to have standard deductions made from the debtor's earnings and paid to the authority.[47] This is known as an attachment of earnings order (AEO). Practice Note No. 9 advises that AEOs are a practical, and in many cases preferable, alternative to distress. The decision to use this method of recovery is a discretionary one. The authority should advise the debtor of its proposed use and give her or him the opportunity to make representations. The authority must consider all the relevant factors before deciding to adopt this method.

The order

The form of the AEO is specified in the regulations.[48] A Welsh language version has also been prescribed.[49] The order should be addressed to, and may be served upon, 'any person who has the debtor in his or her employment'. It does not have to be addressed to a person by name. A copy should also be sent to the debtor. The order must specify:

- the fact that a liability order has been obtained against the debtor and the outstanding sum;
- the rate at which deductions are to be made from net earnings by reference to the relevant tables in the regulations (Exhibit 12.3, p160); *and*
- the period within which each deduction made is to be paid to the authority, ie within 19 days of the end of the month in which the deduction is made.

The order must be signed by the proper officer of the authority. Practice Note No. 9 advises that a facsimile signature is acceptable.

How long does the order last?

Once an AEO has been made it remains in force until:

- the whole amount to which it relates has been paid; *or*
- it is cancelled by the issuing authority.[50]

The authority may cancel the order on its own initiative or following an application by the debtor or the debtor's employer.[51]

The debtor's duties

While an attachment of earnings order is in force, the debtor must notify the authority in writing of each occasion when s/he:

- leaves an employment; *or*
- becomes employed or re-employed.[52]

The notification must include:

- the name and address of the employer;
- the debtor's work or identity number in the employment; *and*
- a statement of earnings from the job; and the deductions from earnings in respect of:
  - income tax,
  - primary Class 1 national insurance contributions,
  - a superannuation scheme.[53]

This notification must be given within 14 days of the day on which the debtor leaves or commences or recommences the employment, or (if later) the day on which s/he is informed by the authority that the order has been made.[54] Failure on the part of the debtor to comply with these duties without reasonable excuse is an offence.[55] The debtor is liable on summary conviction to a fine not exceeding level 2 on the standard scale.[56] If the debtor makes a statement which s/he knows to be false on a relevant point or recklessly makes a statement which is false on a relevant point the debtor is also guilty of an offence and is liable on summary conviction to a fine not exceeding level 3 on the standard scale.[57]

The employer's duties and rights

The person on whom the order is served, and who employs the debtor, must comply with the order.[58] If the employer does not comply with the order s/he is guilty of an offence and liable to a fine unless it can be shown that all reasonable steps were taken to comply with the order.[59] A person guilty of this offence is liable to a fine not exceeding level 3 on the standard scale.[60]

Additionally the employer must:

- tell the authority within 14 days if the person who is the subject of the order is not in her/his employment;
- inform the authority, within 14 days, of the date the debtor ceased to be employed;[61]
- tell the debtor/employee the total deductions made under the order at the same time as the pay statement is issued or if there is no such statement as soon as possible after the deduction is made.[62]

Employers must also tell the authority within 14 days, of the date that the debtor enters their employment and they become aware that an AEO is in force, or alternatively tell the authority on the day on which they become aware that an AEO exists.[63] The employer is guilty of an offence and liable to a fine if s/he:

- fails to provide the required notification without reasonable excuse; *or*
- makes a statement which s/he knows to be false in a relevant point; *or*
- recklessly makes a statement which is false in a relevant point.[64]

A person guilty of the first offence is liable to a fine not exceeding level 2 the standard scale. A person guilty of the other offences is liable to a fine not exceeding level 3 on the standard scale.[65]

In addition to each amount deducted under the AEO the employer is able to deduct a further £1 towards administration costs.

The deductions to be made

The deductions under an AEO are made from the debtor's net earnings in accordance with standard tables contained in the regulations (Exhibit 12.3). The deduction to be made depends on the payment period. The daily earnings table is used where earnings are not weekly, monthly or some permutation of weeks and months, or earnings are irregular. Special rules cover more unusual payment arrangements. The debtor, authority and employer can agree to a lower deduction than the statutory amount. The employer should alter the deductions if the employee's earnings change.

Earnings are defined as sums payable to the debtor by way of wages or salary. This includes any fees, bonus, commission, overtime pay or other emoluments payable in addition to wages or salary or payable under a contract of service. It also includes statutory sick pay.[66] The following are not treated as earnings:

- sums payable by any public department of the Government of Northern Ireland or of a territory outside the United Kingdom;
- pay or allowances payable to the debtor as a member of Her Majesty's forces;
- allowances or benefit payable under the Social Security Acts;
- allowances payable in respect of disablement or disability;
- wages payable to a person as a seaman, other than wages payable to him as a seaman of a fishing boat.[67]

While AEOs cannot be made on the pay of armed services personnel because their pay is not considered to be earnings, the Army Act 1955, the Air Force Act 1955 and the Naval Discipline Act 1957 contain provisions which allow certain officers authorised by the Defence Council to make compulsory deductions from the pay of a member of the armed services. Crown employees, eg civil servants, can be subject to AEOs. The chief officer of a department, office or other body is treated as the employer and the net earnings paid by the Crown are treated as attachable earnings.[68]

Net earnings are defined as the gross earnings payable minus:

- income tax;
- employee Class 1 national insurance contributions;
- amounts deducted towards a superannuation scheme; *and*
- amounts deducted under an AEO made under the Community Charges (Administration and Enforcement) Regulations 1989

Exhibit 12.3   Deductions made under an attachment of earnings order

Deductions from weekly earnings

Net earnings	Deduction rate %
Not exceeding £35	0
Exceeding £35 but not exceeding £65	3
Exceeding £65 but not exceeding £90	5
Exceeding £90 but not exceeding £110	7
Exceeding £110 but not exceeding £175	12
Exceeding £175 but not exceeding £250	17
Exceeding £250	17 in respect of the first £250 and 50 in respect of the remainder

Deductions from monthly earnings

Net earnings	Deduction rate %
Not exceeding £152	0
Exceeding £152 but not exceeding £260	3
Exceeding £260 but not exceeding £360	5
Exceeding £360 but not exceeding £440	7
Exceeding £440 but not exceeding £700	12
Exceeding £700 but not exceeding £1,000	17
Exceeding £1,000	17 in respect of the first £1,000 and 50 in respect of the remainder

Deductions based on daily earnings

Net earnings	Deduction rate %
Not exceeding £5	0
Exceeding £5 but not exceeding £9	3
Exceeding £9 but not exceeding £13	5
Exceeding £13 but not exceeding £16	7
Exceeding £16 but not exceeding £25	12
Exceeding £25 but not exceeding £36	17
Exceeding £36	17 in respect of the first £36 and 50 in respect of the remainder

where that order was made before the council tax order in question.[69]

Priority of AEOs

There is a priority for AEOs where more than one has been made against the same individual.[70] Council tax attachment orders should be dealt with one at a time and in the order in which they are made. Where an order under the Attachment of Earnings Act 1971 or the Child Support Act 1991 is already in force then a council tax order should not be met. Where a council tax order is in effect when a 1971 or 1991 Act order is made the council tax order should continue to be met and the balance is considered attachable for the other order.[71]

Practice Note No. 9 advises that where a 1971 or 1991 order is for maintenance (and therefore the likelihood of the council tax AEO being actioned in the foreseeable future is remote) the employer should be encouraged to return the council tax order to the authority so that a different recovery method can be considered. In such cases the authority should cancel the council tax AEO.

When may an elected member's allowances be attached?

This recovery option is new for the purposes of council tax. It applies to elected members of a billing or precepting authority other than members of the Common Council of the City of London or the Receiver for the Metropolitan Police District.[72] The decision to use this method of recovery is a discretionary one. The authority should advise the debtor of its proposed use and give her/him the opportunity to make representations. The authority must consider all the relevant factors before deciding to adopt this method.

The authority can make an order under which it can deduct 40 per cent from that member's attendance allowances (including allowances for attending conferences and other meetings), and from basic and special responsibility allowances where they are paid in accordance with a scheme made under s18 of the Local Government and Housing Act 1989 and s175 of the Local Government Act 1972.

Once an order has been made it remains in force until:

* the whole amount to which it relates has been paid; *or*
* it is cancelled by the issuing authority.[73]

The authority may cancel the order on its own initiative or following an application by the debtor.

Restrictions on voting

If an elected member in England, Wales or Scotland fails to pay an amount of council tax within two months of the due date s/he may not vote on any matter which influences the setting of the authority's council tax or in England and Wales a precepting authority's precept.[74] The member must disclose this fact at any meeting where this rule applies. Members who fail to comply with this rule are on summary conviction liable to a fine not exceeding level 3 on the standard scale unless they prove that they did not know that this rule applied to them at the time of the meeting or the matter in question was the subject of consideration at the meeting. In England and Wales prosecutions may only be commenced with the permission of the Director of Public Prosecutions.[75]

When may deductions be made from income support?

Where a liability order in England and Wales, or a summary warrant or a decree in Scotland, has been obtained against the debtor, the authority may apply to the Secretary of State for Social Security, ie the local Benefits Agency office making the income support payments, for deductions to be made from that benefit.[76] The decision to use this method of recovery is a discretionary one. The authority should advise the debtor of its proposed use and give her/him the opportunity to make representations. The authority must consider all the relevant factors before deciding to adopt this method.

Though many council taxpayers on income support receive 100 per cent council tax benefit this is not the case:

- where they are jointly liable with someone other than a married or unmarried partner; *or*
- where there is a non-dependant in the household.

Deduction from income support may also be pursued by the authority where the taxpayer was liable to pay council tax prior to income support entitlement.

The maximum weekly amount that can be deducted is 5 per cent of the personal allowance for a single claimant aged 25 or over, ie £2.20 per week in 1993–94. Deductions are not possible:

- where there is not enough benefit in payment to allow a deduction; *or*

- where there are higher priority deductions for other debts such as rent, fuel or water.

The application

To obtain the deduction the authority must supply the following information to the local Benefits Agency office:

- the name and address of the debtor;
- the name and address of the authority making the application;
- the name and place of the court which made the liability order or granted the summary warrant or decree;
- the date on which the liability order was made or the summary warrant or decree granted;
- the amount specified in the liability order, summary warrant or decree; *and*
- the total sum which the authority wish to have deducted from income support.[77]

Deductions from income support may be made in respect of only one application from the authority at any given time. If a second application is made before the sum specified in the first application has been fully recovered, the second has to wait until the first has been cleared.[78]

Determining the application

Within 14 days of receipt of the application, or as soon as practicable after that, an adjudication officer at the local Benefits Agency office should determine whether or not there is sufficient entitlement to income support to enable any deduction to be made. Deduction should only be made if:

- the amount of income support payable after any such deduction is 10 pence or more a week; *and*
- the total amount payable under that and similar deductions, for example for fuel, rent etc, does not exceed an amount equal to three times 5 per cent of the personal allowance for a single claimant aged 25 years or over, ie £6.60 a week in 1993–94.[79]

The debtor and the authority should be notified of the decision in writing within 14 days of it having been made. The debtor should also be notified of her or his appeal rights against the adjudication officer's decisions. The local Benefits Agency office should make the deductions so long as:

- the debtor is entitled to income support throughout any benefit week; *and*
- no deductions are being made in respect of the debtor for council tax or community charge arrears under any other application.[80]

Payment of deductions to the authority

Payments of sums deducted from income support should be made to the authority concerned, as far as is practicable, at intervals not exceeding 13 weeks.[81]

End of deductions

Deductions should end if:

- there is no longer sufficient entitlement to income support to enable a deduction to be made; *or*
- the authority withdraws its application for deductions to be made; *or*
- the debt is discharged.[82]

Where the whole of the amount to which the deductions relate has been paid, the authority must give notice of that fact to the local Benefits Agency office within 21 days or as soon as practicable after that.[83]

Provision of information to the debtor

The local Benefits Agency office must notify the debtor in writing of the total sums deducted under any application:

- on receipt of a written request for such information from the debtor; *or*
- on the termination of deductions made under any such application.[84]

When may bankruptcy or winding-up proceedings be initiated?

Where a liability order has been obtained the (outstanding) amount on the liability order is a debt for the purposes of:

- bankruptcy proceedings under s267 of the Insolvency Act 1986 where the debtor is an individual; *or*
- winding-up proceedings under ss122(1)(f) or 221(5)(b) where the debtor is a registered or unregistered company.[85]

This means that the authority can apply to bankrupt an individual, but only if s/he owes at least £750 (the authority can combine all the debts owed to it, eg community charge, council rents and council tax), or wind up a company. The court makes an order following a hearing of the petition. In the event of bankruptcy or winding-up proceedings occurring no other recovery action can be taken. This does not affect the bankrupt individual's ongoing council tax liability. In addition preferential creditors such as the Inland Revenue and Customs and Excise may take all the available funds. An individual facing bankruptcy proceedings should obtain professional advice as quickly as possible. A useful and free plain English guide to bankruptcy is produced by the Insolvency Service of the Department of Trade and Industry.[86]

When may a charging order be obtained?

This method is available where the debtor is the owner or part-owner of the dwelling. It is not relevant if the debtor is a tenant or licensee. The authority, if it has obtained a liability order and the debt outstanding is at least £1,000, may apply to the county court for a charging order against the debtor's dwelling if it is the one that gave rise to the council tax arrears.[87] The decision to use this method of recovery is a discretionary one. The authority should advise the debtor of its proposed use and give her/him the opportunity to make representations. The authority must consider all the relevant factors before deciding to adopt this method.

In deciding whether to grant a charging order the county court must:

- consider the personal circumstances of the debtor; *and*
- whether any other person would be unduly prejudiced if an order were granted.[88]

A charging order effectively 'mortgages' the property with the debt. If the debt remains unpaid the authority may apply to the court for the property to be sold to pay the debt. In practice the court rarely orders the property to be sold. Obtaining a charging order does mean, however, that, if the property is sold, the authority is potentially entitled to receive the outstanding amount from the proceeds of the sale. This is only the case, however, if there are sufficient funds remaining after any charge with a higher priority, such as a building society mortgage, has been met.

When is a debtor sent to prison?

In England and Wales the authority may, in certain circumstances, apply to the magistrates' court for the issue of a warrant committing the debtor to prison.[89] If either before, or after, the issuing of a warrant the amount in question is paid or offered to the authority it must accept the amount concerned and no further action should be taken.[90]

An application for the issue of such a warrant may only be made if:

- the debtor is an individual aged 18 or over;
- the authority has sought to levy distress; *and*
- the person attempting to levy has reported to the authority that s/he was unable (for whatever reason) to find any or sufficient goods on which to levy the amount.[91]

This includes cases where a bailiff has been unable to obtain entry. Where a liability order has been made against joint taxpayers a warrant of commitment may not be applied for unless the authority has sought to levy distress against all of them and the person making the distress reports to the authority that, in relation to each of them, s/he was unable to find any or sufficient goods.[92]

Practice Note No. 9 advises that an authority which has not attempted any remedy other than distress should satisfy itself, by looking again at any information it holds on the debtor, that none of the other available remedies would prove more effective. Many magistrates are reluctant to issue a committal warrant unless all relevant recovery methods have been attempted.

The court must enquire into the debtor's means in her/his presence before issuing a warrant of commitment.[93] To enable such an enquiry to take place a justice of the peace (but not a justices' clerk)[94] may issue a summons requiring the debtor to appear before a magistrates' court and/or issue a summons for the debtor's arrest.[95] A warrant of commitment is only issued if the court is satisfied that failure to pay is due to the debtor's:

- wilful refusal; *or*
- culpable neglect.[96]

The maximum period of imprisonment is three months[97] but the court may, and normally does, postpone the issue of a warrant for such time and on such conditions as it decides.[98] These conditions normally include the debtor entering into an agreement to pay the amount outstanding. If the court decides not to issue a warrant, or fix a term of imprisonment, it may remit all or part of the amount due.[99]

In *R v Faversham and Sittingbourne Justices, ex parte Ursell*,[99a] it was held that justices who had fixed a term of imprisonment for wilful refusal to pay the community charge but postponed the issue of a warrant on condition of future payment in instalments must hold a further hearing before issuing a warrant of commitment to prison following breach of the condition.

The debtor must be given notice of the date and time of that further hearing and an opportunity to attend. The debtor may wish to put the authority to proof of non-payment and is entitled to draw the court's attention to any change in circumstances since the decision to fix a term of imprisonment was made which rendered it inexpedient for the warrant of commitment to be issued. Mr Justice Schiemenn decided that, though there was no explicit power within the relevant regulations, there had to be an inherent power in the court to vary its own order in a case where, since the decision was made, the debtor had become, for instance, incapable of earning by reason of an accident. In *R v St Albans Justices, ex parte George Pointer*,[99b] it was established that the test to be applied on the second hearing is whether there has been wilful refusal or culpable neglect. The case of *R v Northampton Magistrates' Court, ex parte Newell*,[99c] confirmed that justices could issue a warrant committing the defaulter to prison for breach of the conditions when s/he is not present in court providing that the defaulter had been given notice of the hearing.

Where a person has been committed to prison and:

- the whole of the amount outstanding is paid – s/he should be released;
- part of the amount outstanding is paid – her/his sentence is reduced on a proportionate basis.[100]

The liability, including the liability of someone who is jointly liable,[101] must be written off after a warrant of commitment has been issued as no further recovery action can be taken in relation to the relevant amount.[102]

What is the statutory enforcement process in Scotland?

Reminders and loss of right to pay by instalments

Where an instalment under the statutory instalment scheme or any special agreement has not been paid by the due date the authority must serve a reminder notice on the liable person. The reminder notice requires payment to be made within seven days.[103] It must include:

- a note of the instalments required to be paid;
- a statement informing the taxpayer that if no, or insufficient, payment is made to cover any instalments that are, or will become, due within seven days of the issue of the reminder the right to pay by instalments is lost and the full year's tax becomes payable after a further seven days.

If two such reminders have been issued during the financial year, although the taxpayer pays up, s/he becomes liable for the whole of the outstanding amount following a third failure to pay without the need for another reminder.[104] The taxpayer should be informed of the consequences of a third failure to pay on the second reminder notice.[105]

The authority may take recovery action where any sum which has become payable to the authority has not been paid.[106] Additionally where elected members of a local authority are in arrears of at least two months there are restrictions on their ability to vote on specific matters – see above.[107]

Summary warrant or decree

If council tax, council water charge or civil penalties are owing then the authority can apply to the sheriff's court for a summary warrant or seek a decree granted in an action of payment. Recovery is normally by way of the summary warrant which offers special accelerated enforcement procedures. The sheriff, on an application by the authority accompanied by a certificate, is automatically obliged to grant a summary warrant in a form provided for by Act of Sederunt.[108] The certificate must contain the following:

- a statement that the persons specified in the application have not paid the sums due;
- a statement that the authority has served a final notice on each such person requiring her/him to make payment of the amount due within 14 days beginning with the day on which the notice was served;
- a statement that that period has expired without full payment;
- a statement that in respect of each of the persons on the application either
  - a period of 14 days has passed without the person initiating an appeal against the authority (Chapter 13) because s/he is aggrieved by the authority's decision that the dwelling is a

chargeable dwelling, or that the person is liable to pay the tax in respect of the dwelling or by the calculation of the amount which must be paid including entitlement to a disability reduction or a discount; *or*

- that the authority has notified the person in question that it believes the grievance is not well founded, or that steps have been taken to deal with the grievance, or two months have passed since the service of the aggrieved person's notice;

• a statement of the amount unpaid by each person.[109]

Where two or more people are jointly liable the authority may seek a warrant which shows those persons as jointly liable or individually liable for the outstanding sum.[110]

Defects in procedure

The legislation seeks to close the door on some of the arguments based on defects in procedure which were successfully employed by solicitors acting for those in arrears with the community charge. In any proceedings for the recovery of any council tax, etc, whether by summary warrant or otherwise, no one is entitled to found upon failure by the levying authority or any other authority to comply with any time limit for action set out in regulations to allow recovery of arrears, etc.[111] Also no misnomer or inaccurate description of any person or place or mistake or informality in any notice or other document or communication relating to the levy or collection of any council tax or council water charge or in any proceedings for the arrears is allowed to prejudice the recovery of the amount in question.[112]

Debtor's duty to supply information

Where a summary warrant or decree for payment has been granted the debtor is under an obligation to provide specified information required by the authority.[113] This obligation relates to information which is the debtor's possession or control and which has been requested by the authority. The obligation lasts for as long as any part of the relevant amount remains unpaid. The information in question is:

• the name of any employer of the debtor;
• the address of the employer's premises at or from which the debtor works;
• where there are no such premises in Scotland, the address of any one place of business of the employer within Scotland;

- the debtor's national insurance number;
- the name of any bank having a place of business in Great Britain with which the debtor maintains an account either in her/his own name or with another;
- the address of the office at which any such account is maintained and, if that office is outside Scotland, the address of the principal office in Scotland, or (if none) in Great Britain, of the bank in question;
- the number of any such account;
- the name and address of any other person or persons who are jointly liable with the debtor to make payment of the whole or any part of the amount in respect of which the warrant or decree was granted.

The information must be supplied in writing within 14 days of the day on which the request is made by the authority.[114] Failure to comply with the request may result in the imposition of a civil penalty.

Deductions from income support

Where an authority has obtained a summary warrant or a decree against the debtor and the debtor is entitled to income support it may also apply to the Secretary of State for deductions to be made from the debtor's income support as described above.

Other recovery methods

The summary warrant authorises recovery of the unpaid council tax, council water charge and civil penalties and a surcharge of 10 per cent of the amount owing by any of the following diligences:

- a poinding and sale in accordance with Schedule 5 to the Debtors (Scotland) Act 1987;
- an earnings arrestment;
- an arrestment and action of furthcoming and sale.[115]

Enforcement of the summary warrant is by sheriff's officers. Their fees and expenses in connection with execution of the warrant are chargeable against the debtor.[116]

Under the summary warrant procedure it is not necessary to apply for a warrant for sale or to notify the debtor of the intention to proceed to poinding or sale.

Poinding and sale

This involves the seizure and sale of the debtor's goods. Most authorities only use this method as a last resort. Schedule 5 to the Debtors (Scotland) Act 1987 specifies a range of items that are exempt from poinding (Exhibit 12.4).

Exhibit 12.4   Articles exempt from poinding

The following articles belonging to a debtor are exempt from poinding:

- clothing reasonably required for the use of the debtor or any member of her or his household;
- implements, tools of trade, books or other equipment reasonably required for the use of the debtor or any member of her or his household in the practice of the debtor's or such member's profession, trade or business, not exceeding in aggregate value £500;
- medical aids or medical equipment reasonably required for the use of the debtor or any member of her or his household;
- books or other articles reasonably required for the education or training of the debtor or any member of her or his household not exceeding in aggregate value £500;
- toys for the use of any child who is a member of the debtor's household;
- articles reasonably required for the care or upbringing of a child who is a member of the debtor's household.

The following articles belonging to a debtor are exempt from poinding if they are at the time of the poinding in a dwelling and are reasonably required for the use in the dwelling of the person residing there or a member of her or his household:

- beds or bedding;
- household linen;
- chairs or settees;
- tables;
- food;
- lights or light fittings;
- heating appliances;
- curtains;

continued

Exhibit 12.4 *continued*

- floor coverings;
- furniture, equipment or utensils used for cooking, storing or eating food;
- refrigerators;
- articles for cleaning, mending or pressing clothes;
- articles used for cleaning the dwelling;
- furniture used for storing:
  - clothing, bedding or household linen
  - articles used for cleaning the dwelling or
  - utensils used for cooking or eating food;
- articles used for safety in the dwelling;
- tools used for maintenance or repair of the dwelling or of household articles.

An earnings arrestment

A sheriff's officer serves on the debtor's employer an earnings' arrestment schedule. This requires the debtor's employer to deduct from the debtor's net earnings on every pay day an amount in accordance with Schedule 2 to the Debtors (Scotland) Act 1987 (Exhibit 12.5). The arrestment remains in effect until either the debt has been paid in full or the debtor stops working for the employer.

An arrestment and action of furthcoming or sale

Arrestment is the process by which money or goods held by a third party for the debtor, may be frozen. It could be applied, for example, to money held by a bank for the debtor in her or his bank account. An arrestment is made by serving a Schedule of Arrestment on the arrestee. This is done by an officer of the court in the presence of one witness. Arrestment freezes the funds. They cannot be withdrawn until the debt has been settled. Usually the debtor is asked to sign a mandate authorising a release of funds equal to the arrears and costs, to the levying authority. Any money that remains in the account is released. Where a mandate is not signed the levying authority must raise an action of furthcoming to allow arrested funds to be transferred to the authority. The debtor cannot defend the action by disputing the debt but s/he can defend it by showing that the arrestment was invalid, procedurally irregular or caught nothing.

Exhibit 12.5 Deductions made under earnings arrestment

Deductions from weekly earnings

Net earnings	Deduction
Not exceeding £35	Nil
Exceeding £35 but not exceeding £40	£1
Exceeding £40 but not exceeding £45	£2
Exceeding £45 but not exceeding £50	£3
Exceeding £50 but not exceeding £55	£4
Exceeding £55 but not exceeding £60	£5
Exceeding £60 but not exceeding £65	£6
Exceeding £65 but not exceeding £70	£7
Exceeding £70 but not exceeding £75	£8
Exceeding £75 but not exceeding £80	£9
Exceeding £80 but not exceeding £85	£10
Exceeding £85 but not exceeding £90	£11
Exceeding £90 but not exceeding £95	£12
Exceeding £95 but not exceeding £100	£13
Exceeding £100 but not exceeding £110	£15
Exceeding £110 but not exceeding £120	£17
Exceeding £120 but not exceeding £130	£19
Exceeding £130 but not exceeding £140	£21
Exceeding £140 but not exceeding £150	£23
Exceeding £150 but not exceeding £160	£26
Exceeding £160 but not exceeding £170	£29
Exceeding £170 but not exceeding £180	£32
Exceeding £180 but not exceeding £190	£35
Exceeding £190 but not exceeding £200	£38
Exceeding £200 but not exceeding £220	£46
Exceeding £220 but not exceeding £240	£54
Exceeding £240 but not exceeding £260	£63
Exceeding £260 but not exceeding £280	£73
Exceeding £280 but not exceeding £300	£83
Exceeding £300	£83 in respect of the first £300 plus 50 per cent of the remainder

continued

Exhibit 12.5 *continued*

Deductions from monthly earnings

Net earnings	Deduction
Not exceeding £152	Nil
Exceeding £152 but not exceeding £170	£5
Exceeding £170 but not exceeding £185	£8
Exceeding £185 but not exceeding £200	£11
Exceeding £200 but not exceeding £220	£14
Exceeding £220 but not exceeding £240	£18
Exceeding £240 but not exceeding £260	£22
Exceeding £260 but not exceeding £280	£26
Exceeding £280 but not exceeding £300	£30
Exceeding £300 but not exceeding £320	£34
Exceeding £320 but not exceeding £340	£38
Exceeding £340 but not exceeding £360	£42
Exceeding £360 but not exceeding £380	£46
Exceeding £380 but not exceeding £400	£50
Exceeding £400 but not exceeding £440	£58
Exceeding £440 but not exceeding £480	£66
Exceeding £480 but not exceeding £520	£74
Exceeding £520 but not exceeding £560	£82
Exceeding £560 but not exceeding £600	£90
Exceeding £600 but not exceeding £640	£98
Exceeding £640 but not exceeding £680	£109
Exceeding £680 but not exceeding £720	£121
Exceeding £720 but not exceeding £760	£133
Exceeding £760 but not exceeding £800	£145
Exceeding £800 but not exceeding £900	£180
Exceeding £900 but not exceeding £1,000	£220
Exceeding £1,000 but not exceeding £1,100	£262
Exceeding £1,100 but not exceeding £1,200	£312
Exceeding £1,200 but not exceeding £1,300	£362
Exceeding £1,300	£362 in respect of the first £1,300 plus 50 per cent of the remainder

continued

Exhibit 12.5 *continued*

Deductions based on daily earnings

Net earnings	*Deduction*
Not exceeding £5	Nil
Exceeding £5 but not exceeding £6	£0.15
Exceeding £6 but not exceeding £7	£0.30
Exceeding £7 but not exceeding £8	£0.45
Exceeding £8 but not exceeding £9	£0.60
Exceeding £9 but not exceeding £10	£1.00
Exceeding £10 but not exceeding £11	£1.20
Exceeding £11 but not exceeding £12	£1.40
Exceeding £12 but not exceeding £13	£1.60
Exceeding £13 but not exceeding £14	£1.80
Exceeding £14 but not exceeding £15	£2.00
Exceeding £15 but not exceeding £17	£2.40
Exceeding £17 but not exceeding £19	£2.70
Exceeding £19 but not exceeding £21	£3.20
Exceeding £21 but not exceeding £23	£3.70
Exceeding £23 but not exceeding £25	£4.30
Exceeding £25 but not exceeding £27	£5.00
Exceeding £27 but not exceeding £30	£6.00
Exceeding £30 but not exceeding £33	£7.00
Exceeding £33 but not exceeding £36	£8.50
Exceeding £36 but not exceeding £39	£10.00
Exceeding £39 but not exceeding £42	£11.50
Exceeding £42	£11.50 in respect of the first £42 plus 50 per cent of the remainder

Enforcement costs

The sheriff's officer's fees, together with the outlays necessarily incurred in connection with the execution of a summary warrant are chargeable against the debtor. No fees, however, are chargeable by the sheriff's officer against the debtor for collecting, and accounting to the authority for the sums paid to him by the debtor in satisfaction of an amount owing to the authority by way of council tax or council water charge.

CHAPTER THIRTEEN

Appeals

This chapter explains:

- what valuation tribunals and valuation appeal committees are;
- which matters may be referred to such tribunals or committees;
- how appeals are made;
- how appeals are dealt with; *and*
- the possibility for further appeals.

What are valuation tribunals and valuation appeal committees?

In England and Wales appeals are dealt with by valuation tribunals. In Scotland appeals are dealt with by the valuation appeal committee. Both types of appeal body are expected to conduct themselves in a more informal and less intimidating way than a court of law.

Valuation tribunals

Valuation tribunals are the renamed valuation and community charge tribunals[1] which among other matters continue to deal with residual appeals on community charge issues.

Valuation tribunals are independent of the authority and the valuation office agency. Most counties have one or two tribunals. A number of valuation tribunals exist in metropolitan areas – London has five. The tribunal usually visits each authority in its area on a rotating basis. The tribunal often uses the authority's premises for hearings. The address of the relevant tribunal's office should be available from the local valuation office and the authority.

Members of a tribunal are local people serving in a voluntary capacity. They are appointed by the relevant county council or metropolitan borough. Members do not necessarily have any particular professional qualifications. The members elect a president who has overall responsibility for the arrangements relating to appeals and for ensuring that appeals are carried out in accordance with the legislation. The members also elect a number of chairpersons.

The tribunal is advised on matters of law and procedure by its clerk who is a salaried employee of the tribunal. The clerk is also the appellant's point of contact with the tribunal. The clerk should be able to respond to requests for advice on procedures, etc, in advance of the hearing. S/he cannot, however, advise on the substance of the appeal.

Valuation appeal committees

In Scotland appeals are dealt with by valuation appeal committees.[2] The model scheme for the constitution of a valuation appeal committee, and the valuation panel of members from which any particular committee is drawn, is contained within SI 1975 No. 1220 The Valuation (Local Panels and Appeal Committees Model Scheme) (Scotland) Order. The panel is made up of local people appointed by the appropriate Sheriff Principal. It consists of a chairperson and three to six ordinary members. Members are unpaid and independent of the assessor and the authority. The committee is assisted by a paid secretary who is usually a lawyer.

On which matters can an appeal be made?

Appeals may be made to a tribunal in England and Wales or a committee in Scotland on:

- valuation matters;
- liability;
- completion notices; *and*
- penalties.

Disagreements over entitlement to a transitional reduction or council tax benefit do not go to the tribunal or committee but to the authority's review board as described in Chapters 9 and 10. Also, in relation to England and Wales, the legislation makes explicit that the following matters may only be dealt with by way of judicial review in the High Court:

- the specification of exempt dwellings in an order by the Secretary of State;
- a determination by the authority to prescribe a class of dwellings where the owner rather than the resident is liable (authorities have not been given this power at the time of writing);

- any determination made by a Welsh authority to give a smaller or no discount on certain furnished property that is no one's sole or main residence;
- any of the calculations made by a billing authority under ss32–37 or 60 of the Local Government Finance Act 1992;
- any of the calculations made by a major precepting authority under ss43–51 or 61 of the Local Government Finance Act 1992;
- the setting of an original or substitute council tax; *and*
- decisions regarding an original or substitute precept.

Do payments have to be made if there is an outstanding appeal?

A person on whom a bill (demand notice) has been served must make the payments required by the bill or any subsequent special agreement reached with the authority. The fact that an appeal has been made does not affect this obligation though some authorities are willing to suspend recovery action until an appeal has been dealt with. If an appeal is upheld any overpayment of tax should be refunded or credited against a future liability.

The one exception to the rule requiring payment even if an appeal has been made is where it has been made against a penalty imposed by the authority. In such cases the penalty does not have to be paid until the appeal has been decided.

How is an appeal made on a valuation matter?

Chapter 3 describes the way in which an interested person may make a proposal to the listing officer or assessor to alter the valuation list. Standard forms for the making of proposals are available from the valuation office or the assessor.

Where the listing officer or assessor considers the proposal to be invalid, but the interested person disagrees, the listing officer or assessor must refer the matter to the appropriate valuation tribunal or valuation appeal committee within four weeks as described in Chapter 3. If the listing officer or assessor disagrees with the proposed alteration s/he must refer the matter to the tribunal or committee within six months from the date on which the proposal was first served. Again this process is described in Chapter 3.

How is an appeal made on a liability issue?

Appeals can be made by an aggrieved person under this heading where there is disagreement with the authority's decision:

- that a dwelling is not exempt (Chapter 5);
- that someone is, or is not, a liable person (Chapter 6);
- that a disability reduction should not be granted (Chapter 7); or
- that a discount should not be granted (Chapter 8).

As with appeals on valuation issues there are two stages to appeals on liability issues. This time the first stage involves writing to the authority not the listing officer or assessor.[3] The letter should state the decision which is disagreed with and the reason or reasons for the disagreement. The authority has two months in which to consider these matters and may ask for additional information. A further appeal may be made to a tribunal or committee if the authority:

- rejects the appeal;
- makes some changes but fails to satisfy the person making the representations; or
- fails to make a decision within the two-month period.[4]

England and Wales

In England and Wales an appeal to a tribunal must normally be made:

- within two months of the date the authority notified the aggrieved person of its decision; or
- within four months of the date when the initial representation was made if the authority has not responded.[5]

The president of the tribunal has the power to allow an out of time appeal where the aggrieved person has failed to meet the appropriate time limit for reasons beyond her/his control.[6]

An appeal is made by the aggrieved person, or someone acting on her/his behalf, writing directly to the clerk of the relevant tribunal. The appeal letter should state:

- the reasons for the appeal;
- the date on which the first letter regarding the matters was served on the authority; and
- the date, if any, s/he was notified by the authority of its decision.[7]

Appeal forms that request the required information are available from the relevant tribunal's office. The clerk should notify the appellant within two weeks that the appeal request has been received. The clerk should also send a copy of the appeal letter or form to the authority.[8]

Where someone is considered by more than one authority to be resident in its area and therefore liable for the tax s/he may appeal against the decisions and may choose one of the relevant valuation tribunals to hear the appeal.[9] The appellant should write to the clerks of the relevant tribunals informing them of her/his decision.

Scotland

In Scotland an appeal to the committee must be made by writing again to the authority within four months of the date on which the grievance was first raised with it in writing.[10] There is no power to consider out of time appeals. The letter should state:

- the reasons for the appeal; *and*
- the date on which the first letter disputing the matters was served on the authority.[11]

The authority must pass the appeal to the secretary of the relevant valuation appeal panel.[12]

How is an appeal made against a penalty?

The authority has power to impose a penalty in certain instances where someone is required to provide information but fails to provide it or provides information which s/he knows to be false. While the matter may be discussed with the authority and it has the power to withdraw the penalty an appeal can be made to a tribunal or a committee.

England and Wales

In England and Wales an appeal to a tribunal must normally be made within two months of the penalty being imposed or in the case of a penalty imposed before 12 March 1993 before 12 May 1993.[13] The president of the tribunal has the discretion to allow an out of time appeal where the aggrieved person has failed to meet the time limit for reasons beyond her/his control.[14] The appeal is made by the aggrieved person, or someone acting on her/his behalf, writing directly to the clerk of the tribunal. The letter should state:

- the reasons for the appeal; *and*
- the date, if any, s/he was notified by the authority of the penalty.[15]

Appeal forms which request the required information are available from the relevant tribunal's office. The clerk should notify the appellant within two weeks that the appeal request has been received. The clerk should also send a copy of the appeal letter or form to the authority.[16]

Scotland

In Scotland an appeal to the committee must be made by writing again to the authority within two months of the penalty being imposed or 1 April 1993 – whichever is the later date.[17] There is no power to consider out of time appeals. The letter should state:

- the reasons for the appeal;
- the date, if any, s/he was notified by the authority of the penalty.[18]

The authority must pass the appeal to the secretary of the relevant valuation appeal panel.[19]

How is an appeal made against a completion notice?

In England and Wales the authority, and in Scotland the assessor, may issue a completion notice that states the date on which a newly erected or structurally altered property is considered to be a dwelling. While the matter can be discussed with the authority or the assessor an appeal can be made to a tribunal or committee.

England and Wales

In England and Wales an appeal to a tribunal must normally be made within four weeks of the notice having been sent.[20] The president of the tribunal may, however, allow an out of time appeal where the aggrieved person has failed to meet this time limit for reasons beyond her/his control.[21]

The appeal is made by the aggrieved person, or someone acting on her/his behalf, writing directly to the clerk of the tribunal.[22] The letter should state the reasons for the appeal and be accompanied by a copy of the completion notice. Appeal forms that request the required information are available from the relevant tribunal's office. The clerk should notify the appellant within two weeks that the appeal request has been received. The clerk should also send a copy of the appeal letter or form to the authority.[23]

Scotland

In Scotland an appeal to the valuation assessment committee must be made by the aggrieved person writing to the assessor within 21 days from receipt of the completion notice.[24] There is no power to consider out of time appeals. The letter should state the reasons for the appeal and be accompanied by a copy of the completion notice.[25] The assessor must pass the appeal to the secretary of the relevant valuation appeal panel.[26]

How are appeals dealt with?

While there are many similarities in the way in which the Scottish valuation assessment committee and the English and Welsh valuation tribunal deal with appeals different rules apply in Scotland from those which apply in England and Wales.[27] Additionally in England and Wales there are a number of differences between the way in which the tribunal deals with appeals on valuation matters from the way in which it deals with appeals on other council tax issues.[28]

An appeal is normally dealt with by way of an oral hearing but if all the parties agree it can be dealt with by way of a written representation.[29] Additionally in England and Wales disputes which would otherwise be the subject of an appeal to a valuation tribunal may be referred to arbitration if all the parties give their written agreement to this way of dealing with the matter.[30]

Withdrawal of appeals

In England and Wales if the listing officer decides after the appeal has been initiated that the proposal is well-founded s/he may withdraw the appeal by writing to the clerk to the tribunal. Also the appellant may withdraw an appeal on a valuation matter by writing to the listing officer who should notify the clerk to the tribunal accordingly.[31]

In Scotland an appeal may be withdrawn by the appellant writing to the secretary of the committee or at the hearing by asking the permission of the committee. If the assessor decides, after the appeal has been initiated, to agree to the original proposal or the authority decides not to contest the appeal it is considered to be withdrawn.[32]

Written representations

Practice Note No. 6 (para 7.1) describes the ability to deal with disputes by way of written representation as providing a relatively quick and effective procedure for resolving straightforward appeals. For an appeal to be dealt with in this way all the parties (normally the appellant, the listing officer/assessor or the authority) must give their written agreement.[33]

There is no maximum time limit in which the tribunal or committee must determine the appeal on the basis of written representations. Once it is agreed that the appeal is to be dealt in this way all parties have four weeks in which to send in their written cases. Copies of these submissions are sent to the other parties. There is then a further four-week period in which comments may be made on these submissions. At the end of this last period the clerk or secretary sends the available material to the tribunal or committee.

The tribunal or committee on receipt of the referral may:

- require any party to provide additional material;
- order that the appeal be dealt with by a hearing; *or*
- go on to reach a decision.[34]

Where additional information is required copies of that material must again be provided to all the other parties. Each party may, within four weeks of receiving the additional material, supply a further statement in response.[35]

In Scotland permission to deal with the appeal by way of written representation may be withdrawn by any of the parties at any time before a decision is reached. This might happen, for example, if the other party's arguments are not as expected. Where permission for the matter to be dealt with by way of written representations has been withdrawn the appeal must be dealt with by way of an oral hearing.[36]

Arbitration in England and Wales

In England and Wales the appellant and the other parties may agree in writing that the appeal be dealt with by way of arbitration rather than by way of a tribunal hearing or by the tribunal considering written representations. Arbitration proceedings are governed by the Arbitration Act 1950. The advantages of arbitration are that proceedings are always in private and that the arbitrator may have much more specialist knowledge of the subject-matter than tribunal members. In any arbitration the award may include any order which could have been made by a tribunal.[37] Either party may seek a judicial review by the High Court of the arbitration award.

Pre-hearing review

In the case of an English or Welsh valuation appeal the tribunal chairperson may order a pre-hearing review with the aim of clarifying the issues to be dealt with at the hearing.[38] This may be done either at the request of the appellant, any other party or on the chairperson's own initiative. At least four weeks' notice must be given of such a pre-hearing.

How much notice should be given of the hearing?

In England and Wales where the appeal is to be dealt with at a hearing the clerk to the tribunal must give at least four weeks' written notice of the date, time and place of the hearing.[39] In Scotland the secretary to the committee must give not less than 35 days' written notice.[40] There is no maximum time limit in which the tribunal or committee must hear the appeal.

In England and Wales the clerk must advertise the date, time and place of the hearing:

- at the tribunal's office; *and*
- outside an office earmarked by the authority for this purpose; *or*
- in another place within the authority's area.[41]

In Scotland the secretary must advertise the details at an office of the authority and the place the hearing will take place if different.[42]

In all cases the advert must name a place where a list of the appeals to be heard may be inspected by members of the public.[43]

Who is disqualified from participating in the hearing?

Natural justice refers to the rules and procedures to be followed by any body including a tribunal or committee that has the duty of adjudicating upon disputes. One of the principles of natural justice is the rule against bias. This requires that someone should not take part in a hearing if a reasonable person would think that that person's participation is likely to lead to bias. In England and Wales the following people are explicitly excluded from participation as a member, clerk or officer of a tribunal in relation to a particular appeal:

- an elected member of the authority in which the dwelling is situated;
- the appellant's spouse; *or*
- someone who supports the appellant financially.[44]

Someone is not disqualified, however, simply because s/he is a member of a local authority, for example a county council, which derives its revenue directly or indirectly from council tax payments that may be affected by the exercise of her/his functions.[45] Where the appellant is an employee or member of the relevant tribunal, her/his appeal is dealt with by another tribunal appointed for that purpose by the Secretary of State.[46]

Representatives

Any party may:

- represent themselves; *or*
- be represented by a lawyer; *or*
- be represented by anyone else.[47]

In England and Wales someone who is representing themselves may have the assistance of someone else, for example, a friend, a relative or a welfare rights adviser.[48] Members of the tribunal or the panel from which the valuation committee is drawn are not permitted to represent parties at its hearings.[49] Additionally in England and Wales employees of the tribunal are also barred from acting in that capacity. In Scotland the committee may, if it is satisfied that there are good and sufficient reasons for doing so, refuse to permit a particular person to represent a party at a hearing.[50]

How is the hearing conducted?

In England and Wales a hearing or determination of an appeal is dealt with by three members of the tribunal one of whom must be a chairperson, and a chairperson must preside. Where all parties that attend the hearing agree the appeal may be decided by two members of a tribunal and in the absence of a chairperson.[51] In Scotland the minimum number of people that constitute a valid committee is three.[52]

Public hearing

The hearing normally takes place in public. In England and Wales the tribunal can decide to hold the hearing in private if any of the parties requests it and the tribunal considers that the interests of that party would be prejudicially affected if the hearing was held in public.[53] In Scotland the committee may, if it has reasonable cause, hold the hearing in private.[54]

Failure to appear

In Scotland if either the appellant or any representative, and in England and Wales if the appellant and any party other than the listing officer fail to appear at the hearing the appeal may be dismissed.[55]

In England and Wales if a party can show reasonable cause for the non-appearance they may request the tribunal to review its decision (see below).[56] In Scotland if the appellant has reasonable excuse for the absence the committee may set a new date, time and place for the hearing.[57] It must give all parties at least seven days' notice. For a hearing to be recalled in this manner the appellant must write to the committee – normally within 14 days of being notified that the original appeal was dismissed – requesting a new hearing date and setting out the reason for the original absence. If the committee consider that there are special circumstances the committee may allow an out of time request.

If any party does not appear at the hearing the tribunal may hear and determine the appeal in its absence.

Order of the hearing

The tribunal or committee may determine the order of the hearing, ie which party puts its case first. Parties at the hearing may examine any witness and call witnesses. The tribunal or committee may require any witness to give evidence by oath or affirmation.[58]

Adjournment

A hearing may be adjourned for such time, to such place and on such terms (if any) as the tribunal or committee thinks fit. Reasonable notice of the time and place to which the hearing has been adjourned must be given to every party.

What evidence can be presented at the hearing?

Where facts, such as the value of a dwelling, are in dispute each party to the hearing should provide evidence that supports its view of the facts. The rules relating to evidence are significantly different between Scotland and England and Wales. The rules that apply in England and Wales are considered first.

England and Wales

The tribunal is not bound by any rules relating to the admissibility of evidence before courts of law, rather it is concerned with the weight of any evidence.[59] For example, what someone else has been heard to say (hearsay) would be admissible at a hearing but given less weight than the direct evidence of a witness. Certain evidence, however, may not be used at the hearing unless the required notice has been given to the appellant and any other party by the authority or listing officer as appropriate.

In a non-valuation appeal the authority must give the other parties two weeks' notice if it wishes to produce evidence of information supplied in connection with a disability reduction or information in relation to liability obtained under Schedule 2 to the Local Government Finance Act 1992. These items of information may be inspected and copies taken by the appellant if at least 24 hours' notice is given to the authority.[60] In a valuation appeal the listing officer must give at least two weeks' notice of information s/he proposes to use at the hearing. Again the appellant and any other party to the appeal may, having given 24 hours' notice, inspect the documents and if desired make a copy of the whole document or an extract from the documents concerned.[61] The listing officer may inform the appellant that s/he wishes to use evidence based on the Inland Revenue's confidential records of sale prices of similar houses. If this is the case the appellant has the right to inspect the relevant documents and to call for information relating to a maximum of four comparable dwellings or, if the listing officer specifies more, the same number as are specified by the officer. The listing officer has the duty of producing both sets of documents at the hearing.[62]

Scotland

In Scotland the committee may require a party to provide the other parties by a set date with:

- a written statement outlining the evidence to be given at the hearing; *and*
- copies of all documents which are to be produced for the hearing.[63]

Where a committee has made such a requirement no other material may be produced unless the committee allows it.[64]

Where there is to be a hearing the committee has the power to grant to any of the parties the same rights of access to documents as could be granted, or provided, by the Court of Session.[65] The committee may require:

- someone's attendance at the hearing as a witness; *or*
- the production of any document relating to the appeal.[66]

Where someone fails to comply with such a written requirement s/he is liable on summary conviction to a fine not exceeding level 1 on the standard scale.[67] No one need produce any material or answer any questions which s/he would be entitled on the grounds of privilege or confidentiality to refuse to produce or answer if the proceedings were in a court of law.[68] This would apply to professional confidences. Additionally, where someone is required to appear as a witness at the hearing and it takes place more than ten miles from her/his home s/he does not have to appear unless the necessary expenses are paid or offered by the committee or the party that required the witness's attendance.[69]

Decisions and orders

In England and Wales where there are only two members and they are unable to agree, the matter must be referred by the clerk to a tribunal consisting of three different members.[70]

Following a hearing the tribunal or committee has the discretion to give an oral decision to the parties concerned. Whether or not an oral decision is given a written decision together with a statement of reasons must be supplied to the parties. In England and Wales this should be done as soon as is reasonably practicable after the decision has been made.[71] In Scotland it must be done within seven days of the decision being given.[72] After the tribunal or committee has made a decision it has the power to make orders to give effect to its decision.

Can decisions be reviewed?

In England and Wales, except where a decision has been the subject of an appeal to the High Court, the tribunal may review its decision or set it aside. This may only be done following a written application from any of the parties on the grounds that:

- the decision was wrongly made due to a clerical error;
- a party did not appear and can show reasonable cause for the non-appearance;
- the decision is affected by a decision of, or on appeal from, the High Court or the Lands Tribunal; *or*
- in relation to a decision on a completion notice new evidence has become available – unless it could have been ascertained by reasonably diligent inquiry or foreseen previously.

An application for a review or set aside should normally be made within four weeks of the day on which written notice of the tribunal's decision was given. The tribunal has the discretion to hear an out of time request for a review or a set aside. Where a listing officer applies to a tribunal for the review of a decision s/he must as soon as reasonably practicable thereafter, notify the authority of the application. So far as is reasonably practicable, the tribunal appointed to review a decision should consist of the same members as the tribunal that took the original decision. If a tribunal sets aside a decision the matter may be reheard or reconsidered by either the same tribunal or a differently constituted one.

As soon as reasonably practicable after the outcome of the request for a review is known the clerk to the tribunal must write to the applicant and every other party to the appeal informing them of the outcome. Additionally where an appeal to the High Court remains undetermined the clerk must also notify the High Court as soon as reasonably practicable after the decision has been made.

What records are kept of decisions?

In Scotland each party has an explicit right to make a recording of the hearing at its own expense. The committee should be informed of the intention to make a recording before the hearing begins.[73]

In England and Wales the clerk has the explicit duty to make arrangements for each of the tribunal's decisions, etc, to be recorded. The records may be kept in any form, whether documentary or otherwise. The record must contain the following information:

- the appellant's name and address;
- the matter appealed against;
- the date of the hearing or determination;
- the names of the parties who appeared (if any);
- the decision of the tribunal and its date;
- the reasons for the decision;
- any order made in consequence of the decision;
- the date of any such order;
- any certificate setting aside the decision;
- any revocation.

A copy, in documentary form, of the relevant entry in the record must, as soon as reasonably practicable after the entry has been made, be sent to each party to the appeal to which the entry relates. Each record must be retained for six years.[74]

Anyone may, at a reasonable time stated by, or on behalf of, the tribunal concerned and without making payment, inspect the records. If without reasonable excuse a person having custody of records intentionally obstructs someone from inspecting the records s/he is liable on summary conviction to a fine not exceeding level 1 on the standard scale.

The member who presided at the hearing or determination of an appeal may authorise the correction of any clerical error in the record; and a copy of the corrected entry must be sent to the persons to whom a copy of the original entry was sent.

Is there any further appeal?

After the tribunal or committee there is no further appeal except on a point of law, ie where the law has been interpreted incorrectly. In England and Wales this is made to the High Court. In Scotland to the Court of Session. The appellant, listing officer, assessor and authority all have an equal right of appeal. The appellant is advised to seek legal advice before embarking upon this course of action. Legal aid may be available.

In England and Wales where the listing officer appeals to the High Court s/he must also notify the authority of the appeal as soon as reasonably practicable. The Court may award costs against the unsuccessful party.

In England and Wales an appeal on a point of law should normally be made within four weeks of:

- the date on which notice is given of the decision or order;
- the date of a decision following review; *or*
- a determination by a tribunal that it will not review its decision where the application for review was made within four weeks of the original decision.

Where the tribunal or committee has acted in breach of natural justice, ie there has not been a fair hearing or there has been some bias in the proceedings, an application for judicial review may also be made.

Council tax legislation (England and Wales)

The Local Government Finance Act 1992

SI 1992 No. 548	The Council Tax (Discount Disregards) Order 1992
SI 1992 No. 549	The Council Tax (Chargeable Dwellings) Order 1992
SI 1992 No. 550	The Council Tax (Situation and Valuation of Dwellings) Regulations 1992
SI 1992 No. 551	The Council Tax (Liability for Owners) Regulations 1992 amended by SI 1993 No. 151
SI 1992 No. 552	The Council Tax (Additional Provisions for Discount Disregards) Regulations 1992 amended by SI 1992 No. 2942 and SI 1993 No. 149
SI 1992 No. 553	The Council Tax (Contents of Valuation Lists) Regulations 1992
SI 1992 No. 554	The Council Tax (Reductions for Disabilities) Regulations 1992 amended by SI 1993 No. 195
SI 1992 No. 558	The Council Tax (Exempt Dwellings) Order 1992 amended by SI 1992 No. 2941 and SI 1993 No. 150
SI 1992 No. 612	The Local Authorities (Calculation of Council Tax Base) Regulations 1992 amended by SI 1992 No. 1742 and SI 1993 No. 196
SI 1992 No. 613	The Council Tax (Administration and Enforcement) Regulations 1992 amended by SI 1992 No. 3008
SI 1992 No. 1741	The Council Tax (Administration and Enforcement) (Attachment of Earnings Order) (Wales) Regulations
SI 1992 No. 1742	The Local Authorities (Calculation of Council Tax Base) (Amendment) Regulations
SI 1992 No. 2428	The Local Authorities (Funds) (England) Regulations 1992

SI 1992 No. 2429	The Billing Authorities (Alteration of Requisite Calculations) (England) Regulations 1992
SI 1992 No. 2904	The Local Authorities (Calculation of Council Tax Base) (Supply of Information) Regulations 1992
SI 1992 No. 2941	The Council Tax (Exempt Dwellings) (Amendment) Order 1992
SI 1992 No. 2942	The Council Tax (Additional Provisions for Discount Disregards) (Amendment) Regulations 1992
SI 1992 No. 3008	The Council Tax (Administration and Enforcement) (Amendment) Regulations 1992
SI 1992 No. 3023	The Council Tax (Prescribed Classes of Dwellings) (Wales) Regulations 1992
SI 1992 No. 3239	The Billing Authorities (Anticipation of Precepts) Regulations 1992
SI 1993 No. 22	The Local Government Finance (Miscellaneous Provisions) (England) Order 1993
SI 1993 No. 149	The Council Tax (Additional Provisions for Discount Disregards) (Amendment) Regulations 1993
SI 1993 No. 150	The Council Tax (Exempt Dwellings) (Amendment) Order 1993
SI 1993 No. 151	The Council Tax (Liability for Owners) (Amendment) Regulations 1993
SI 1993 No. 175	The Council Tax (Transitional Reduction Scheme) (England) Regulations 1993 amended by SI 1993 No. 253
SI 1993 No. 191	The Council Tax and Non-Domestic Ratings (Demand Notices) (England) Regulations 1993
SI 1993 No. 195	The Council Tax (Reductions for Disabilities) (Amendment) Regulations 1993
SI 1993 No. 196	The Council Tax (Administration and Enforcement) (Amendment) Regulations 1993
SI 1993 No. 253	The Council Tax (Transitional Reduction Scheme) (England) (Amendment) Regulations 1993
SI 1993 No. 255	The Council Tax (Demand Notices) (Wales) Regulations 1993
SI 1993 No. 290	Council Tax (Alteration of Lists and Appeals) Regulations 1993
SI 1993 No. 292	Valuation and Community Charge Tribunals (Amendment) Regulations 1993
SI 1993 No. 494	Council Tax (Deduction from Income Support) Regulations 1993
SI 1993 No. 615	The Valuation and Community Charge Tribunals (Amendment) (No. 2) Regulations 1993

Council tax legislation (Scotland)

The Local Government Finance Act 1992

SI 1992 No. 1203	The Council Water Charge (Scotland) Regulations 1992
SI 1992 No. 1329	The Council Tax (Valuation of Dwellings) (Scotland) Regulations 1992
SI 1992 No. 1330	The Council Tax (Contents of Valuation Lists) (Scotland) Regulations 1992
SI 1992 No. 1331	The Council Tax (Liability of Owners) (Scotland) Regulations 1992
SI 1992 No. 1332	The Council Tax (Administration and Enforcement) (Scotland) Regulations 1992
SI 1992 No. 1333	The Council Tax (Exempt Dwellings) (Scotland) Order 1992
SI 1992 No. 1334	The Council Tax (Dwellings) (Scotland) Regulations 1992
SI 1992 No. 1335	The Council Tax (Reduction for Disabilities) (Scotland) Regulations 1992
SI 1992 No. 1408	The Council Tax (Discounts) (Scotland) Order 1992
SI 1992 No. 1409	The Council Tax (Discounts) (Scotland) Regulations 1992
SI 1992 No. 2796	The Council Tax (Exempt Dwellings) (Scotland) Amendment Order 1992
SI 1992 No. 2955	The Council Tax (Dwellings and Part Residential Subjects) (Scotland) Regulations 1992
SI 1992 No. 3024	The Local Government (District Council Tax) (Scotland) Regulations 1992
SI 1992 No. 3290	The Council Tax (Administration and Enforcement) (Scotland) Amendment Regulations 1992
SI 1993 No. 277	The Council Tax (Transitional Reduction Scheme) (Scotland) Regulations 1993 amended by SI 1993 No. 527
SI 1993 No. 342	The Council Tax (Discounts) (Scotland) Amendment Regulations 1993
SI 1993 No. 343	The Council Tax (Discounts) (Scotland) Amendment Order 1993

SI 1993 No. 344	The Council Tax (Liability of Owners) (Scotland) Amendment Regulations 1993
SI 1993 No. 345	The Council Tax (Exempt Dwellings) (Scotland) Amendment Order 1993
SI 1993 No. 354	The Council Tax (Valuation of Dwellings) (Scotland) Amendment Regulations 1993
SI 1993 No. 355	The Council Tax (Alteration of Lists and Appeals) (Scotland) Regulations 1993
SI 1993 No. 526	The Council Tax (Dwellings) (Scotland) Regulations 1993

Council tax Practice Notes

England and Wales

PN No. 1   Valuation Lists
PN No. 2   Liability, Discounts and Exemptions
PN No. 3   Council Tax Benefit
PN No. 4   Transitional Arrangements
PN No. 5   Administration (including Billing and Collection)
PN No. 6   Appeals
PN No. 7   Tax Setting, Precepting and Levying
PN No. 8   Data Protection
PN No. 9   Recovery and Enforcement

Wales

PN A   The Council Tax in Wales
PN B   Tax Setting, Precepting and Levying in Wales

Notes

Chapter 1: Overview

1 EW Act s 1
2 S Act ss 70, 97(1)–(2)
3 S Act s 97(3) Sch 2 para 19

Chapter 2: Dwellings

1 EW Act s 4(1)(2); S Act s 72(6)
2 EW Act s 2(2)(a); S Act s 71(2)(a)
3 EW Act s 3
4 EW Act s 19
5 EW SI 1992 No. 550
6 Ibid
7 EW SI 1992 No. 549
8 Ibid
9 S Act s 72
10 S SI 1992 No. 2955 (S 242)
11 S SI 1992 No. 1334 (S 131)
12 Ibid
13 S SI 1992 No. 1333 (S 130)
14 S SI 1992 No. 2955 (S 242)
15 S SI 1993 No. 526 (S 63)
16 S Act s 72(8) and Sch 5
17 S SI 1992 No. 2955 (S 242)
18 EW Act s 17 Sch 4A to the Local Government Finance Act 1988 as amended; S Act s 83(1) Sch 6
19 S Act Sch 6
20 EW SI 1993 No. 290 Reg 5; S SI 1993 No. 355 (S 39) Reg 5

Chapter 3: Valuation

1 EW Act s 20
2 EW Act s 26
3 S Act s 84(1)
4 S Act s 86(5)
5 S Act s 86(10)
6 EW Act s 21; S Act s 86(7)
7 EW Act s 21; S Act s 86(8)
8 EW Act s 21; S Act s 86(9)
9 EW Act s 26; S Act s 89
10 Ibid
11 EW Act s 27; S Act s 90
12 Ibid
13 Ibid
14 EW Act s 26; S Act s 90
15 Ibid
16 EW Act s 21 and SI 1992 No. 550; S Act s 86(2) and SI 1992 No. 1329 (S 126)
17 EW SI 1992 No. 550 Reg 6; S SI 1992 No. 1329 (S 126) Reg 2
18 Ibid
19 EW SI 1992 No. 550 Reg 7
20 S SI 1992 No. 1329 (S 126) Reg 3
21 EW Act s 22; S Act s 84
22 Ibid
23 EW Act s 22; S Act s 85
24 EW Act s 22; S Act s 84
25 EW Act s 2(2)(b); S Acts 71(2)(b)
26 EW Act s 23 and SI 1992 No. 553; S Act s 84 and SI 1992 No. 1330
27 EW Act s 23; S Act s 84
28 EW Act s 28; S Act s 91
29 Ibid
30 EW SI 1993 No. 290; S SI 1993 No. 355 (S 39)
31 EW Act s 24; S Act s 87
32 Ibid
33 EW SI 1992 No. 550; S SI 1992 No. 1329 as amended by SI 1993 No. 354 (S 38)
34 EW SI 1993 No. 290 Reg 2; S SI 1993 No. 355 (S 39) Reg 3
35 EW SI 1993 No. 290 Reg 5
36 EW SI 1993 No. 290 Reg 5; S SI 1993 No. 355 (S 39) Reg 5
37 S SI 1993 No. 355 (S 39) Reg 5

38 Ibid
39 EW SI 1993 No. 290 Reg 5; S SI 1993
    No. 355 (S 39) Reg 5
40 Ibid
41 Ibid
42 Ibid
43 Ibid
44 Ibid
45 EW SI 1993 No. 290 Reg 6; S SI 1993
    No. 355 (S 39) Reg 6
46 Ibid
47 EW SI 1993 No. 290 Reg 6
48 EW SI 1993 No. 290 Reg 35; S SI
    1993 No. 355 (S 39) Reg 6
49 EW SI 1993 No. 290 Reg 7
50 S SI 1993 No. 355 (S 39) Reg 7
51 S SI 1993 No. 355 (S 39) Reg 12
52 EW SI 1993 No. 290 Reg 8; S SI 1993
    No. 355 (S 39) Reg 8
53 EW SI 1993 No. 290 Reg 8
54 Ibid
55 Ibid
56 S SI 1993 No. 355 (S 39) Regs 8–9
57 S SI 1993 No. 355 (S 39) Reg 10
58 EW SI 1993 No. 290 Reg 9
59 EW SI 1993 No. 290 Reg 10
60 EW SI 1993 No. 290 Reg 12
61 EW SI 1993 No. 290 Reg 13
62 Ibid
63 EW SI 1993 No. 290 Reg 11
64 Ibid
65 S SI 1993 No. 355 (S 39) Reg 14
66 S SI 1993 No. 355 (S 39) Reg 15
67 Ibid
68 Ibid
69 Ibid
70 S SI 1993 No. 355 (S 39) Reg 11
71 EW SI 1993 No. 290 Reg 15; S SI
    1993 No. 355 (S 39) Reg 16
72 EW SI 1993 No. 290 Reg 15
73 Ibid
74 S SI 1993 No. 355 (S 39) Reg 16
75 Ibid
76 EW Act s 29; S Act s 92

Chapter 4: The amount of tax

1 EW Act s 38; S Act s 96
2 E Act s 5(2)
3 S Act s 74(2)

4 W Act s 5(3)
5 EW Act s 5(1); S Act s 74(1)
6 EW Act s 2; S Act s 71
7 See eg E SI 1993 No. 1480; W SI 1993
   No. 1608
8 EW Act s 66(2)(d)

Chapter 5: Exempt dwellings

1 EW Act s 4(2); S Act s 72(6)
2 EW Act s 2(2)(a); S Act 71(2)(a)
3 S Act s 72(6)–(7) and para 7(2)–(3) of
   Sch 11, SI 1992 No. 1333 as amended
   by SI 1992 No. 2796 and SI 1993 No.
   345
4 SI 1993 No. 150
5 SI 1992 No. 558
6 Class A SI 1992 No. 558 as amended
   by SI 1993 No. 150
7 Ibid
8 Class B SI 1992 No. 558
9 Class C SI 1992 No. 558 as amended
   by SI 1993 No. 150
10 Class D SI 1992 No. 558 as amended
   by SI 1993 No. 150
11 EW Act s 6
12 Class E SI 1992 No. 558
13 Class I SI 1992 No. 558
14 Class J SI 1992 No. 558
15 Class F SI 1992 No. 558 as amended
   by SI 1993 No. 150
16 Class G SI 1992 No. 558
17 Class H SI 1992 No. 558
18 Class L SI 1992 No. 558
19 Class O SI 1992 No. 558 as amended
   by SI 1992 No. 2941
20 PN No. 2 para 30
21 Class P SI 1992 No. 558 as amended
   by SI 1992 No. 2941
22 Class Q SI 1992 No. 558 as amended
   by SI 1993 No. 150
23 Class K SI 1992 No. 558 as amended
   by SI 1993 No. 150
24 Class M SI 1992 No. 558
25 Class N SI 1992 No. 558 as amended
   by SI 1993 No. 150
26 PN No. 2 p28
27 S SI 1992 No. 1333 as amended by SI
   1992 No. 2796 and SI 1993 No. 345
28 S SI 1992 No. 1333 (S 130) Sch para 1

29 S SI 1992 No. 1333 (S 130) Sch para 2
30 S SI 1992 No. 1333 (S 130) Sch para 3
31 S SI 1992 No. 1333 (S 130) Sch para 4
32 S SI 1992 No. 1333 (S 130) Art 2
33 S SI 1992 No. 1333 (S 130) Sch para 5
    as amended by SI 1992 No. 2796
34 S SI 1992 No. 1333 (S 130) Sch para 6
35 S SI 1992 No. 1333 (S 130) Sch para 7
36 S SI 1992 No. 1333 (S 130) Sch para 8
37 S SI 1992 No. 1333 (S 130) Sch para 9
38 S SI 1992 No. 1333 (S 130) Sch para 10
39 S SI 1992 No. 1333 (S 130) Sch para 14
40 S SI 1992 No. 1333 (S 130) Sch para 15
41 S SI 1992 No. 1333 (S 130) Sch para 16
42 S SI 1992 No. 1333 (S 130) Sch para 18
43 S SI 1992 No. 1333 (S 130) Sch para 23 as inserted by SI 1993 No. 345 (S 37)
44 S SI 1992 No. 1333 (S 130) Sch para 19
45 S SI 1992 No. 1333 (S 130) Sch para 20
46 S SI 1992 No. 1333 (S 130) Sch para 21
47 S SI 1992 No. 1333 (S 130) Sch para 22 as inserted by SI 1992 No. 2796 (S 238)
48 S SI 1992 No. 1333 (S 130) Sch para 13
49 S SI 1992 No. 1333 (S 130) Sch para 11
50 S SI 1992 No. 1333 (S 130) Sch para 12
51 S SI 1992 No. 1333 (S 130) Sch para 17
52 EW A&E Reg 8; S A&E Reg 7
53 EW A&E Reg 9; S A&E Reg 8
54 Ibid
55 EW A&E Reg 10; S A&E Reg 9
56 EW A&E Reg 10 as amended by SI 1992 No. 3008; S A&E Reg 9 as amended by SI 1992 No. 3290
57 S A&E Reg 9 as amended by SI 1992 No. 3290
58 EW A&E Reg 10; S A&E Reg 9

59 Ibid
60 Ibid
61 Ibid
62 EW A&E Reg 11; S A&E Reg 10
63 Ibid
64 EW Act s 14(2) and Sch 3; S Act s 97(4) Sch 3
65 Ibid
66 Ibid
67 Ibid
68 EW Act s 16; S Act s 81
69 Ibid
70 Ibid

Chapter 6: Liability

1   EW Act s 6(2); S Act s 75(2)
2   EW Act s 2(2)(c); S Act s 71(2)(c)
3   EW Act s 6(6)
4   EW Act s 6(5)
5   EW Act ss 6-7
6   Ibid
7   S Act s 75(5)
8   EW Act s 6(5); S Act s 99(1)
9   *City of Bradford MBC v Neil Anderton*, QBD 14 February 1991; *The Times*, 15 February 1991
10 EW Act s 8(1); S Act s 76(1)
11 EW SI 1992 No. 551; S SI 1992 No. 1331 (S 128)
12 EW SI 1992 No. 551 as amended by SI 1993 No. 151; S SI 1992 No. 1331 (S 128) as amended by SI 1993 No. 344 (S 36)
13 EW SI 1992 No. 551 as amended by SI 1993 No. 151
14 EW SI 1992 No. 551; S SI 1992 No. 1331 (S 128)
15 Ibid
16 S SI 1992 No. 1331 (S 128) as amended by SI 1993 No. 344 (S 36)
17 EW Act s 6(3)–(4); S Act s 75(3)–(4)
18 EW Act s 9; S Act s 77
19 EW SI 1992 No. 613 as amended by SI 1992 No. 3008
20 EW Act ss 6(4) and 9(2); S Act ss 75(4) and 77(2)
21 EW Act s 2; S Act s 71
22 EW SI 1992 No. 613 Reg 6; S SI 1992 No. 1332 (S 129) Reg 5

23 EW SI 1992 No. 613 Regs 3,12; S SI 1992 No. 1332 (S 129) Reg 2
24 EW Act s 14(2) Sch 3; S Act s 97(4) Sch 3
25 Ibid
26 Ibid
27 Ibid
28 EW SI 1993 No. 292 Reg 36(3)
29 EW SI 1992 No. 613 Reg 4 as amended by SI 1992 No. 3008; S SI 1992 No. 1332 (S 129) Reg 3 as amended by SI 1992 No. 3290 (S 264)
30 S SI 1992 No. 1332 (S 129) Reg 3
31 EW SI 1992 No. 613 Reg 5; S SI 1992 No. 1332 (S 129) Reg 4
32 EW Act s 16; S Act s 81
33 Ibid
34 Ibid
35 EW SI 1993 No. 292 Reg 36

Chapter 7: Disability reductions

1 EW Act s 13, SI 1992 No. 554 as amended by SI 1993 No. 195
2 S Act s 80(1)–(4),(6)–(7), SI 1992 No. 1335
3 S SI 1992 No. 1335
4 EW SI 1992 No. 550 Reg 6; S SI 1992 No. 1329 (S 126) Reg 2
5 EW Act s 16; S Act s 81
6 Ibid
7 Ibid
8 EW SI 1993 No. 292 Reg 36

Chapter 8: Discounts

1 EW Act s 11; S Act s 79
2 EW Act s 2(2)(d); S Act s 71(2)(d)
3 W Act s 12
4 W SI 1992 No. 3023
5 W Act s 12
6 W Act s 66
7 EW Act s 6; S Act s 99(1)
8 EW Act s 11 Sch 1, SI 1992 No. 548, SI 1992 No. 552, SI 1992 No. 2942; S SI 1992 No. 1408 (S 136), SI 1992 No. 1409 (S 137), SI 1993 No. 342 (S 34), SI 1993 No. 343 (S 35)
9 EW S Act Sch 1 para 3
10 EW SI 1992 No. 552 as amended by

SI 1993 No. 149; S 1992 No. 1409 (S 137)
11 EW S Act Sch 1 para 4
12 EW SI 1992 No. 548; S SI 1992 No. 1408 (S 136)
13 PN No. 2 p28
14 EW SI 1992 No. 548; S SI 1992 No. 1408 (S 136)
15 Ibid
16 Ibid
17 Ibid
18 Ibid
19 EW SI 1992 No. 548
20 Ibid
21 Ibid
22 Ibid
23 Ibid
24 EW S SI 1992 No. 1408 (S 136)
25 Ibid
26 Ibid
27 EW SI 1992 No. 548; S SI 1992 No. 1408 (S 136)
28 EW SI 1992 No. 548; S SI 1408 (S 136) as amended by SI 1993 No. 343 (S 35)
29 EW SI 1992 No. 548; S SI 1408 (S 136)
30 Ibid
31 EW SI 1992 No. 548
32 EW SI 1992 No. 548; S SI 1408 (S 136)
33 Ibid
34 EW S Act Sch 1 para 1; EW SI 1992 No. 548; S SI 1408 (S 136)
35 EW S Act Sch 1 para 1 and SI 1992 No. 548
36 EW S Act Sch 1 para 2; EW SI 1992 No. 548; S SI 1992 1408 (S 136)
37 EW S Act Sch 1 para 6
38 Ibid
39 EW S Act Sch 1 paras 7–8
40 EW Act Sch 1 para 7
41 Ibid
42 S Act Sch 1 para 8
43 EW SI 1992 No. 548
44 S Act Sch 1 para 8
45 EW SI 1992 No. 548
46 S SI 1992 No. 1408 (S 136)
47 EWS Act Sch 1 para 9; EW SI 1992 No. 552; S SI 1992 No. 1409 (S 137)

48 EWS Act Sch 1 para 11; EW SI 1992 No. 552; S SI 1992 No. 1409 (S 137)
49 EW SI 1992 No. 2942; S SI 1993 No. 342 (S 34)
50 EW SI 1992 No. 552; S SI 1992 No. 1409 (S 137)
51 EW SI 1992 No. 613 Reg 14; S SI 1332 (S 129) Reg 12
52 EW SI 1992 No. 613 Reg 15; S SI 1332 (S 129) Reg 13
53 EW SI 1992 No. 613 Reg 16; S SI 1332 (S 129) Reg 15
54 Ibid
55 EW Act s 14(2) Sch 3; S Act s 97(4) Sch 3
56 Ibid
57 Ibid
58 Ibid
59 EW Act s 16; S Act s 81
60 Ibid
61 Ibid

Chapter 9: Transitional reduction

1 EW Act s 13 and SI 1993 No. 175 as amended by SI 1993 No. 253; S Act s 80 and SI 1993 No. 277 (S 25) as amended by SI 1993 No. 527 (S 64)
2 E SI 1993 No. 175 Reg 2(1); S SI 1993 No. 277 (S 25) Reg 2(1)
3 S SI 1993 No. 277 (S 25) Reg 2(1)
4 E SI 1993 No. 175 Reg 5; S SI 1993 No. 277 (S 25) Reg 4
5 E SI 1993 No. 175 Sch 2 Pt II as amended by SI 1993 No. 253
6 E SI 1993 No. 175 Sch 2 Pt I
7 S SI 1993 No. 277 (S 25) Reg 2(1)
8 E SI 1993 No. 175 Reg 4
9 S SI 1993 No. 277 (S 25) Reg 5
10 E SI 1993 No. 175 Sch 1; S SI 1993 No. 277 (S 25) Reg 5
11 E SI 1993 No. 175 Reg 2; S SI 1993 No. 277 (S 25) Reg 2
12 E SI 1993 No. 175 Reg 7
13 E SI 1993 No. 175 Reg 10
14 E SI 1993 No. 175 Reg 11(1); S SI 1993 No. 277 (S 25) Reg 6
15 E SI 1993 No. 175 Reg 12; S SI 1993 No. 277 (S 25) Reg 7

16 E SI 1993 No. 175 Reg 13; S SI 1993 No. 277 (S 25) Reg 8
17 E SI 1993 No. 175 Reg 13(2); S SI 1993 No. 277 (S 25) Reg 8(2)

Chapter 10: Council tax benefit (CTB)

1 EWS Act s131 and Sch 9
2 EWS s131(3) Social Security Contributions and Benefits Act 1992
3 EWS s131(11) Social Security Contributions and Benefits Act 1992
4 Ibid
5 Ibid
6 EWS SI 1992 No. 1814 Reg 40
7 Ibid
8 EWS SI 1992 No. 1814 Reg 38
9 Ibid
10 EWS SI 1992 No. 1814 Reg 40(3)
11 EWS SI 1992 No. 1814 Reg 51
12 EWS SI 1992 No. 1814 Reg 53
13 EWS SI 1992 No. 1814 Reg 60
14 EWS SI 1992 No. 1814 Reg 51
15 EWS SI 1992 No. 1814 Reg 84
16 EWS SI 1992 No. 1814 Reg 51
17 Ibid
18 Ibid
19 Ibid
20 EWS SI 1992 No. 1814 Reg 3
21 EWS SI 1992 No. 1814 Reg 52
22 EWS SI 1992 No. 1814 Reg 4
23 EWS SI 1992 No. 1814 Reg 52
24 Ibid
25 Ibid
26 EWS SI 1992 No. 1814 Part IV
27 EWS SI 1992 No. 1814 Regs 20, 22 and 27 and Sch 3
28 EWS SI 1992 No. 1814 Reg 24 and Sch 4
29 EWS s139 Social Security Administration Act 1992
30 EWS SI 1992 No. 1814 Reg 37
31 EWS SI 1992 No. 1814 Regs 8–9 and Sch 1
32 EWS s131(6) Social Security Contributions and Benefits Act 1992
33 EWS SI 1992 No. 1814 Reg 55
34 EWS SI 1992 No. 1814 Reg 54 and Sch 2

35 EWS SI 1992 No. 1814 Reg 60
36 EWS SI 1992 No. 1814 Reg 54 and Sch 2
37 EWS SI 1992 No. 1814 Reg 54
38 EWS SI 1992 No. 1814 Reg 54 and Sch 2
39 Ibid
40 EWS s 131(9) Social Security Contributions and Benefits Act 1992
41 EWS SI 1992 No. 1909
42 EWS SI 1992 No. 1814 Reg 62
43 EWS SI 1992 No. 1909
44 Ibid
45 EWS SI 1992 No. 1814 Reg 62(16)
46 EWS SI 1992 No. 1814 Reg 58
47 EWS SI 1992 No. 1814 Reg 84
48 EWS SI 1992 No. 1814 Reg 67 and Sch 6 Part VII
49 EWS SI 1992 No. 1814 Reg 67
50 EWS SI 1992 No. 1814 Reg 68
51 EWS SI 1992 No. 1814 Reg 70
52 EWS SI 1992 No. 1814 Reg 68
53 EWS SI 1992 No. 1814 Reg 71

Chapter 11: Bills and payments

1 EW A&E Reg 22; S A&E Reg 18
2 EW A&E Reg 2(3); S A&E Reg 19(2)
3 S A&E Reg 17
4 S A&E Reg 18
5 EW A&E Reg 28A
6 EW A&E Reg 19
7 S A&E Reg 17
8 EW A&E Reg 18; S A&E Reg 19
9 EW A&E Reg 18
10 EW A&E Reg 20; S A&E Reg 20
11 S A&E Reg 20
12 EW A&E Reg 20; S A&E Reg 20
13 EW A&E Reg 17(4)
14 E SI 1993 No. 191; W 1993 No. 255; S A&E Reg 28 and Sch 2
15 E SI 1993 No. 191 Part I Sch 3; W SI 1993 No. 255 Part II Sch 2
16 E SI 1993 No. 191 Reg 4; W SI 1993 No. 255 Reg 5; S A&E Reg 29
17 EW Act s 16; S Act s 81
18 EW A&E Reg 30
19 EW A&E Reg 21 and Sch 1 Part I; S A&E Reg 21 and Sch 1
20 S Act Sch 2 para 19

21 EW A&E Sch 1 Part 1 as amended by SI 1992 No. 3008; S A&E Sch 1
22 Ibid
23 EW A&E Sch 1 Part I; S A&E Sch 1 Part 1
24 Ibid
25 Ibid
26 S Act Sch 2 para 19
27 EW A&E Sch 1 Part II
28 Ibid
29 EW A&E Reg 28
30 EW A&E Sch 1 Part III; S A&E Sch 1 Part II
31 Ibid
32 Ibid
33 Ibid
34 Ibid
35 Ibid
36 EW A&E Reg 21; S A&E Reg 21
37 EW A&E Reg 25; S A&E Reg 24
38 EW A&E Reg 26; S A&E Reg 25
39 EW A&E Regs 24–25; S A&E Regs 23–24
40 EW A&E Reg 24
41 EW A&E Regs 24–25 and 31; S A&E Reg 23–24 and 27
42 Ibid
43 Ibid
44 EW A&E Reg 24; S A&E Reg 23
45 EW A&E Reg 55
46 EW A&E Reg 29; S A&E Reg 26
47 Ibid
48 Ibid
49 Ibid

Chapter 12: Enforcement

1 EW A&E Reg 23
2 Ibid
3 Ibid
4 Ibid
5 EW A&E Reg 33
6 EW A&E Reg 54
7 EW A&E Reg 34
7a QBD, 27 March 1991
8 EW A&E Reg 34
9 *Associated Provincial Picture Houses Ltd v Wednesbury Corporation* [1948] 1 KB 223
10 EW SI 1992 No. 613 Reg 31

11 EW A&E Reg 34
12 EW A&E Reg 53(3)
13 EW A&E Reg 34
14 EW A&E Reg 35
15 EW A&E Reg 34
16 Ibid
16a Court of Appeal, 25 July 1991
17 *R v Leicester City Justices, ex parte Barrow and Another* – Court of Appeal, Lord Donaldson of Lymington, Master of the Rolls, Lord Justice Staughton and Sir Christopher Slade, 25 July 1991
18 EW A&E Reg 34
19 EW A&E Reg 57
20 EW A&E Regs 35 and 48 and Sch 2 Forms A and B
21 EW A&E Reg 36
22 EW A&E Reg 36 as amended by SI 1993 No. 773
23 EW A&E Reg 36
24 Ibid
25 EW A&E Reg 56
26 Ibid
27 EW A&E Reg 52
28 EW A&E Reg 54
29 EW A&E Reg 45(1) and (2)
30 EW A&E Reg 45
31 Ibid
32 EW A&E Reg 52
33 EW A&E Reg 45
34 EW A&E Reg 45(8)
35 EW A&E Reg 45(1A) as inserted by SI 1993 No. 773
36 EW A&E Reg 45
37 EW A&E Sch 5 para 2(2) as amended by SI 1992 No. 613
37a QBD, 12 July 1991
38 EW A&E Reg 45(5)
39 EW A&E Sch 5 para 3(2) as amended by SI 1993 No. 773
40 A consultative document issued by the Public Law Project, Charles Clore House, 17 Russell Square, London WC1B 5DR
41 EW A&E Reg 46(1)
42 EW A&E Reg 53(3)
43 EW A&E Reg 46(2)
44 EW A&E Reg 45(7)
45 EW A&E Reg 46(3)
46 EW A&E Reg 46(4)
47 EW A&E Reg 37
48 EW A&E Sch 3
49 W SI 1992 No. 1741
50 EW A&E Reg 37(2)
51 EW A&E Reg 41
52 EW A&E Reg 40
53 Ibid
54 Ibid
55 EW A&E Reg 56
56 Ibid
57 Ibid
58 EW A&E Reg 37(3)
59 EW A&E Reg 56(2), (3) and (6)
60 EW A&E Reg 56
61 EW A&E Reg 39(4)
62 EW A&E Reg 39(2) and (3)
63 EW A&E Reg 39(6) and (7)
64 EW A&E Reg 56
65 Ibid
66 EW A&E Reg 32
67 Ibid
68 EW A&E Reg 43
69 EW A&E Reg 32(1) as amended by SI 1993 No. 773
70 EW A&E Reg 42
71 Ibid
72 EW A&E Reg 44
73 Ibid
74 EW Act s106; S Act s 112
75 EW Act s106
76 EWS SI 1993 No. 494
77 EWS SI 1993 No. 494 Reg 4
78 EWS SI 1993 No. 494 Reg 8(4)
79 EWS SI 1993 No. 494 Reg 5
80 EWS SI 1993 No. 494 Reg 8
81 EWS SI 1993 No. 494 Reg 8(5)
82 EWS SI 1993 No. 494 Reg 8(3)
83 EWS SI 1993 No. 494 Reg 8(6)
84 EWS SI 1993 No. 494 Reg 8(7)
85 EW A&E Reg 49
86 The Insolvency Service, Room 706, Bridge Place, 88/89 Eccleston Square, London SW1V 1PT (tel: 071-215 0753/4)
87 EW A&E Reg 50(1)-(3)
88 EW A&E Reg 51(1)
89 EW A&E Reg 47(1)
90 EW A&E Reg 47(6)
91 EW A&E Reg 47(1)

92 EW A&E Reg 54
93 EW A&E Reg 47(2)
94 EW A&E Reg 53(3)
95 EW A&E Reg 48(5)
96 EW A&E Reg 47(2)
97 EW A&E Reg 47(7)
98 EW A&E Reg 47(3)(b)
99 EW A&E Reg 48(2)
99a *The Times*, 18 March 1992
99b QBD, 14 July 1992
99c QBD, 15 April 1992
100 EW A&E Reg 47(6)-(8)
101 EW A&E Reg 54
102 EW A&E Reg 52(1)
103 S A&E Reg 22
104 Ibid
105 Ibid
106 S Act s 97 and Sch 8 para 1
107 S Act s 112
108 S Act Sch 8 para 2
109 S A&E Reg 30
110 Ibid
111 S Act Sch 8 para 3
112 Ibid
113 S A&E Reg 31
114 Ibid
115 S Act Sch 8 para 2
116 S Act Sch 8 para 4

Chapter 13: Appeals

1 EW Act s15
2 S Act s81
3 EW Act s16; S Act s81
4 Ibid
5 EW SI 1993 No. 292 Reg 36
6 Ibid
7 EW SI 1993 No. 292 Reg 37
8 Ibid
9 EW SI 1993 No. 292 Reg 35
10 S SI 1993 No. 355 Reg 22
11 Ibid
12 Ibid
13 EW SI 1993 No. 292 Reg 36
14 Ibid
15 EW SI 1993 No. 292 Reg 37
16 Ibid
17 S SI 1993 No. 355 Reg 23
18 Ibid
19 Ibid
20 SI 1993 No. 292 Reg 36
21 Ibid
22 SI 1993 No. 292 Reg 37
23 EW SI 1993 No. 292 Reg 37
24 S SI 1993 No. 355 Reg 24
25 Ibid
26 Ibid
27 EW SI 1993 Nos. 290 and 292; S SI 1993 No. 355
28 EW SI 1993 Nos. 290 and 292
29 EW SI 1993 No. 290 Reg 20, No. 292 Reg 40; S SI 1993 No. 355 Reg 27
30 EW SI 1993 No. 290 Reg 33, No. 292 Reg 52
31 EW SI 1993 No. 290 Reg 19
32 S SI 1993 No. 355 Reg 26
33 EW SI 1993 No. 290 Reg 20, No. 292 Reg 40; S SI 1993 No. 355 Reg 27
34 Ibid
35 Ibid
36 S SI 1993 No. 355 Reg 27
37 EW SI 1993 No. 290 Reg 33, No. 292 Reg 52
38 EW SI 1993 290 Reg 21
39 EW SI 1993 No. 290 Reg 22, No. 292 Reg 41
40 S SI 1993 No. 355 Reg 28
41 EW SI 1993 No. 290 Reg 22, No. 292 Reg 41
42 S SI 1993 No. 355 Reg 28
43 EW SI 1993 No. 290 Reg 22, No. 292 Reg 41; S SI 1993 No. 355 Reg 28
44 EW SI 1993 No. 290 Reg 23, No. 292 Reg 42
45 Ibid
46 EW SI 1993 No. 290 Reg 17, No. 292 Reg 35
47 EW SI 1993 No. 290 Reg 24, No. 292 Reg 43; S SI 1993 No. 355 Reg 34
48 EW SI 1993 No. 290 Reg 24, No. 292 Reg 43
49 EW SI 1993 No. 290 Reg 24, No. 292 Reg 43; S SI 1993 No. 355 Reg 34
50 S 1993 No. 355 Reg 34
51 EW SI 1993 No. 290 Reg 25, No. 292 Reg 44
52 S SI 1975 No. 1220
53 EW SI 1993 No. 290 Reg 25, No. 292 Reg 44
54 S 1993 No. 355 Reg 32

55 EW SI 1993 No. 290 Reg 25, No. 292
   Reg 44; S SI 1993 No. 355 Reg 31
56 EW SI 1993 No. 290 Reg 30, No. 292
   Reg 49
57 S 1993 No. 355 Reg 31
58 EW SI 1993 No. 290 Reg 25, No. 292
   Reg 44; S SI 1993 No. 355 Reg 33
59 EW SI 1993 No. 290 Reg 25, No. 292
   Reg 44
60 EW SI 1993 No. 292 Reg 45
61 EW SI 1993 No. 290 Reg 26
62 Ibid
63 S 1993 No. 355 Reg 29
64 Ibid
65 S 1993 No. 355 Reg 30
66 Ibid
67 Ibid
68 Ibid
69 Ibid
70 EW SI 1993 No. 290 Reg 28, No. 292
   Reg 47
71 Ibid
72 S 1993 No. 355 Reg 36
73 S 1993 No. 355 Reg 35
74 EW SI 1993 No. 290 Reg 31, No. 292
   Reg 50

Index

NATIONAL WELFARE BENEFITS HANDBOOK, 1993/94 edition

In April 1993 the benefit rates and regulations change again. The new **Handbook** is therefore completely revised and updated, with all you need to know about means-tested benefits and how to claim them. There is comprehensive coverage of **income support, housing benefit, family credit, the social fund and disability working allowance,** and of the major changes affecting benefits this year, including: ● the impact of the **Child Support Act** on benefits, including the benefit penalty and deductions for maintenance ● the new **council tax benefit** ● the impact of the new **community care** arrangements on benefits ● direct deductions for mortgage payments and fines. There is information on health and education benefits, other help for people with disabilities, and on how to appeal.

£6.95 (£2.65 for individual benefit claimants — direct from CPAG)

RIGHTS GUIDE TO NON-MEANS-TESTED BENEFITS, 1993/94 edition

Fully revised and updated, this essential, practical companion to the Handbook includes: ● revised coverage of unemployment benefit ● expanded coverage of disability living allowance after a year in operation ● earnings rules and disability benefit ● the contributions system ● statutory sick pay and statutory maternity pay ● pensions and benefits for widows ● industrial injuries and diseases ● benefits administration and how to appeal. The **Rights Guide,** the Handbook and the new Child Support Handbook are all fully cross-referenced and indexed to law, regulations and — where relevant — Commissioners' decisions.

£6.50 (£2.45 for individual benefit claimants — direct from CPAG)

CHILD SUPPORT HANDBOOK, 1st edition: 1993/94

Child maintenance arrangements for benefit claimants change fundamentally in April 1993. The National Welfare Benefits Handbook covers the impact on benefits, but **this new companion volume to the Handbook and Rights Guide provides parents and advisers with definitive, expert guidance on all aspects of the scheme:** the law and its implications for claimants and all other parents affected, including ● who is affected, key terms and how to apply for maintenance ● the Child Support Agency, providing information and the effects on either parent of non-cooperation ● a step-by-step guide to the formula for calculating maintenance ● exemptions, the benefit penalty, collection and enforcement, IS deductions ● shared care, second families, competing applications etc ● Child Support Appeal Tribunals. Fully indexed and cross-referenced to legislation and to its companion volumes, **CPAG's Child Support Handbook will become the standard guide for parents, advisers, social workers, lawyers and anyone else needing to understand the scheme.**

£5.95 (£2.25 for individual benefit claimants — direct from CPAG)

All three CPAG Handbooks are available from April — place your order now as copies are sent on a first come, first served basis.

The CPAG/NACAB **Benefits Poster 1993/94** (A2 size, £1.95) gives you benefit rates at a glance.

Please send me:

_____ **National Welfare Benefits Handbook** @ £6.95 each £ _____

_____ **Rights Guide to N.M.T. Benefits** @ £6.50 each £ _____

_____ **Child Support Handbook** @ £5.95 each £ _____

_____ Benefits Poster @ £1.95 each £ _____

PRICES INCLUDE POSTAGE AND PACKING

I enclose a cheque/PO, payable to **CPAG Ltd** for — Total: £ _____

Name _____

Address _____

_____

_____ Postcode _____

Return this form with your payment to CPAG Ltd, 1-5 Bath Street, London EC1V 9PY

Welfare Rights Bulletin

The Bulletin is essential reading for welfare rights advisers, providing a bi-monthly update and back-up to the CPAG Handbook and Rights Guide, and to the new Child Support Handbook. There is more detailed and comprehensive coverage of social security developments than in any other magazine.

Contents include the fullest coverage of new and significant Commissioners' decisions, as well as: Court judgements, changes in law and practice, news from welfare rights workers and how to tackle common problem areas.

ISSN 0263 2098

£15.00 for a full year's subscription (6 issues)

Sent automatically to CPAG Rights and Comprehensive members, and Bulletin subscribers.

Fuel Rights Handbook

9th edition: 1993-94

Antoinette Hoffland and Nicholas Nicol

The *Fuel Rights Handbook* is completely revised and updated to take account of all significant changes since last year's edition, and in readiness for the imposition of VAT on fuel in 1994.

New features of this edition include:

- expanded coverage of problems with Fuel Direct
- updated information on the problems around pre-payment meters, including how to resist the imposition of pre-payment meters
- the first coverage of how the Competition and Services (Utilities) Act is actually working in practice, plus expanded coverage of provisions that have only recently started to take effect
- updated coverage of the question of liability for electricity (beneficial user)
- revised guidance on theft and tampering issues
- how to use OFFER and OFGAS to resolve disputes
- the latest social security changes from April 1993
- a revised section on multiple debt
- revised and expanded coverage of the position in Scotland
- the new developments in standards of performance by the utilities
- a completely new section covering mobile homes and caravans
- new case law

This edition is essential reading for any adviser dealing with fuel issues.

Please send me _____ copies of the *Fuel Rights Handbook* 1993-94 @ £7.95 each (incl p&p)   £_____

I enclose a cheque/PO for £_____ payable to CPAG Ltd

Name _____

Address _____

_____

_____ Postcode _____

Return order with payment to CPAG Ltd, 1-5 Bath Street, London EC1V 9PY

Ethnic Minorities' Benefits Handbook, 1st edition

Paul Morris, Inderpal Rahal and Hugo Storey
edited by Janet Gurney

CHILD POVERTY ACTION GROUP

This unique *Handbook* bridges the gap between immigration and benefits advisers, giving information and practical guidance on both immigration and benefits rules for anyone entering or leaving the UK. There is a particular focus on the provisions most likely to affect ethnic minority claimants.

The major part of the *Ethnic Minorities' Benefits Handbook* consists of separate chapters on each benefit, interweaving the benefits and immigration issues throughout. There are also key sections devoted to immigration law and EC law.

Fully indexed and cross-referenced to both social security and immigration law, the *Ethnic Minorities' Benefits Handbook* is the only authoritative and up-to-date guide to benefits in this increasingly important area of advice work. It will be revised and updated regularly.

Advisers will find the *Ethnic Minorities' Benefits Handbook* invaluable, as will many claimants – whether they are non-EC immigrants, members of ethnic minorities in the UK, EC citizens in the UK, or UK citizens in other EC countries.

400 pages   0 946744 50 5   £8.95

**Send cheque/PO for £8.95 (incl p&p) to
CPAG Ltd (Pubs/WRB), 1-5 Bath Street, London EC1V 9PY**